Surprised by Hope

Further Meditations on Synodality

Timothy Cardinal Radcliffe

LITURGICAL PRESS
Collegeville, Minnesota

litpress.org

Cover art courtesy of Getty Images.

Library of Congress Control Number: 2025935456

ISBN 979-8-4008-0236-2
ISBN 979-8-4008-0237-9 (e-book)

Contents

Introduction: Yes! Amen!

"Did the Synod on Synodality achieve anything?" That is surely the question that has been asked most often since the end of the second assembly in October 2024. Many people had high hopes that the synod would make decisions that would transform the Church, such as the ordination of women to the diaconate, but it did not do so. Instead it began a process—a word that is typical of Pope Francis—which will be more radically transformative than we can imagine, founded on encounter with the Lord and with his brothers and sisters.

The four meditations with which this book begins were given at the retreat that preceded the synod assembly. They focus on the encounter of the disciples with the Risen Lord in John's gospel: in the garden and the upper room (John 20), and on the beach (John 21). These meditations were intended to prepare us for our encounter with the Lord during the synod, in silence and in prayer, and with each other in conversation and mutual attention—two encounters with the same mystery of love: "Beloved, let us love one another, because love is from God; everyone who loves is born of God and knows God" (1 John 4:7).

We gathered in synod so that together we could walk "the Way," the earliest name of the Church (Acts 9:2). Of course, changes are needed in the structures of the Church, but these will only be life-giving if they spring from our renewed communion with each other in the Lord. Otherwise they will merely be furthering an agenda and the political victory of one ecclesiastical party. Asking what the synod has achieved is not the most helpful question, since the synod is a process of opening ourselves to the guidance of the Spirit, the divine wind which blows where it wills (John 3:8). We have embarked on a journey to the Kingdom that will not end until God's peace reigns and "they will not hurt or destroy on all my holy mountain; for the earth will be full of the knowledge of the Lord as the waters cover the sea" (Isa 11:9). We make this pilgrimage as a sign of hope for a world which is crucified by hatred and seems farther away than ever from Christ's peace.

We came to Rome in October 2024 because we were summoned by the Holy Father. Christianity is a response to God who calls us all to come. This invitation we transmit to each other and to the world:

> The Spirit and the bride say, "Come."
> And let everyone who hears say, "Come."
> And let everyone who is thirsty come.
> Let anyone who wishes take the water of life as a gift.
> (Rev 22:17)

The heart of our Christian life is the word *Amen*. It occurs only 30 times in the Old Testament but 123 times in the New Testament. It is the characteristic word of Jesus. He is the only person, as far as I know, to begin a sentence with the word, and even pronouncing it twice: "Amen, amen, I say to you" (John 1:51, and twenty-four other times).[1] It is the word that sums up the call of Jesus to live and which Saint Jerome advised should never be translated.[2] It is our Yes, one way of translating "Amen."

Jesus is God's "Yes" to us and our "Yes" to God: "For the Son of God, Jesus Christ, whom we proclaimed among you, Silvanus and Timothy and I, was not 'Yes and No'; but in him it is always 'Yes.' For in him every one of God's promises is a 'Yes.' For this reason it is through him that we say the 'Amen,' to the glory of God" (2 Cor 1:19). In the Book of Revelation, it is even the name of Jesus, "the words of the Amen, the faithful and true witness, the origin of God's creation" (3:14).

1. New American Bible, Revised Edition.
2. See Saint Jerome, Epistle 26 to Marcella.

So we gathered in synod to say to the Lord our Yes, responding to the Lord's Yes to us. We may disagree on what that assent should mean in the life of the Church, on what is a faithful development of the tradition and what is a betrayal, but it cannot be denied that we are all called to be ready, with our loins girded, our feet shod, and our staffs in our hands, to set forth for wherever the Lord is leading us.

When Benedict Green, a monk of the Anglican community of Mirfield, England, drew near to his end after years of suffering from Parkinson's disease, he wrote to tell his friends that he was no longer able to welcome them since he could not speak anymore. He concluded with the words of Dag Hammarskjöld (1905–1961), the second secretary general of the United Nations: "For all that has been, Thank you. For all that will be, Yes."

Ever since the Church gathered in Jerusalem in AD 70 to consider on what conditions the Gentiles should be baptized, synods have met so that we could say together our Yes to the Lord. Often this has taken the form of assenting to new ways of articulating our faith. Encounter with the Lord, with other cultures, and with each other rejuvenates the Church, and renews our Yes. Saint John's gospel, with his theology of the Logos, is fresh from the encounter of Hebrew and Greek wisdom. The universities of the thirteenth century forged a new language born of the encounter of Christianity with the Arabic world, and the rediscovered works of Aristotle.

We, too, gathered in the synod to find new ways of saying "Yes" to the Lord who commissions us to say to our contemporaries: "Let everyone who is thirsty come." We beg for new fresh words so that we can, in turn, reach out especially to the millions of young people who are searching for the meaning of their lives: "Come and take the water of life as a gift. There is a place for you at the table." As Pope Francis likes to say, "All, All, All are welcome."

When the assembly ended, we were just at the beginning of finding fresh words of assent and invitation to carry us beyond the sterile battles between so-called traditionalists and progressives. We sought for ways to assent to the Lord's summons in words that are enriched by the encounter of North and South, East and West.

We are just at the beginning of finding fresh words for today's thirsty people. For example, a question that puzzled both assemblies of the synod was how, as women and men, ordained and lay, we are both equal and different. This is a question which young people are posing in almost every part of the world today. On most continents, the relationships between young men and women are uneasy. In the final chapter of the book, I describe how only slowly, largely after the end of the assembly, I became aware that the synod was moving from the language of "complementary," which implies fixed roles, to the dynamic and evolving language of "reciprocity." We are just at the beginning of renewing how we speak to each other in ways that are loving, attentive, and true, and to speak of our God in love and truth.

This is more important today than at any time since I was born, at the end of the Second World War. Today the global order in which I grew up, and which has shaped our world for eighty years, is in danger of crumbling. A symptom of this is a collapse of solidarity. Many wealthy countries, especially in the West, are radically reducing their aid to developing countries. This will result in the deaths of millions of people. It is more than the cessation of a flow of support to those in need. It is the loss of a vision of what it means to be human, and our shared dignity as the children of God, made in the divine image and "what Adam Smith, the great philosopher-economist of the Enlightenment, memorably described as a 'fellow feeling for the suffering of others.' "[3]

At this moment of the breakdown of our solidarity with those who suffer and die, the synod invites us to say a resounding, "Yes, you are our brothers and sisters, flesh of our flesh. Let everyone who is thirsty, come." We also respond as they call us to come and receive their gifts too.

Timothy Cardinal Radcliffe OP
Ash Wednesday 2025

3. Kevin Watkins, "The Assault on Solidarity," *The Tablet*, March 8, 2025.

Searching in the Dark

John 20:1-18

During the retreat last year,[1] we meditated on how to listen to each other. How may we face our differences in hope, opening our hearts and minds to each other? Some barriers did fall, and I hope we began to see those with whom we disagree not as opponents but as fellow disciples, fellow seekers.

This year we have a new focus: "*How* to Be a Missionary Synodal Church."[2] But the foundation of all that we shall do is the same: patient, imaginative, intelligent,

1. See Timothy Radcliffe OP, *Listening Together: Meditations on Synodality* (Liturgical Press, 2024)—Ed.

2. See XVI Ordinary General Assembly of the Synod of Bishops, "*How* to Be a Missionary Synodal Church: *Instrumentum Laboris* for the Second Session (October 2024)," July 9, 2024, https://press.vatican.va/content/salastampa/en/bollettino/pubblico/2024/07/09/240709d.html. Hereafter cited as IL.

open-hearted listening. I even thought of repeating the same talks that I offered at the last retreat, but you might notice! Herbert McCabe OP once told me of a time that he realized at the last moment that he was due to give a lecture to a distinguished theological society. He grabbed a lecture from his files, leapt on his motorbike, and arrived just in time. When he opened his notes, he saw that he had given the same lecture to the same society a year before. "What did you do?" I asked. He replied, "I left out the jokes. They are the only things anyone remembers." Your memories may be better.

Profound listening is still the foundation of everything we shall do this year. It is, the *Instrumentum Laboris* says, "the first act of the Church" (IL 6). The writer Amos Oz said of his grandfather: "He listened. He did not just politely pretend to listen, while impatiently waiting for her to finish what she was saying and shut up. He did not break into his partner's sentence and finish it for her. He did not cut in to sum up what she was saying so as to move on to another subject. He did not let his interlocutress talk into thin air while he prepared in his head the reply that he would make when she finally finished. He did not pretend to be interested or entertained, he really was."[3] Listening to God and to our brothers and sisters is the discipline of holiness.

3. *A Tale of Love and Darkness*, trans. Nicholas de Lang (Vintage, 2005), 110.

This year we shall be reflecting on "the one mission of proclaiming the Risen Lord and his Gospel" (IL, Introduction) to a world that "sit[s] in darkness and in the shadow of death" (Luke 1:79). To guide our meditations, we shall take four resurrection scenes from Saint John's Gospel. I call these four scenes "Searching in the Dark," "The Locked Room," "The Stranger on the Beach," and "Breakfast with the Lord." Each sheds some light on how to be a missionary synodal Church in our crucified world.

Our first scene begins in the night: "Early on the first day of the week, while it was still dark, Mary Magdalene came to the tomb" (John 20:1). This is where we, too, are today. Our world is even more darkened by violence than when we gathered here a year ago. She comes looking for the body of her beloved Teacher. We, too, are gathered in this synod to search for the Lord. In the West, God seems to have largely disappeared. We face not so much atheism but a pervasive indifference. Skepticism poisons the hearts even of many believers. But all Christians everywhere are searchers for the Lord, like Mary Magdalene before dawn.

We, too, in this synod may feel like we are in the dark. Since the last assembly, so many people, including participants in this synod, have expressed their doubts as to whether anything is going to be achieved. Like Mary Magdalene, some say, "Why have they taken away our hope? We expected so much from the synod, but perhaps there will be just more empty words."

But although it is dark, the Lord is already present in the garden with Mary Magdalene and with us. Before his death Jesus said, "Unless a grain of wheat falls into the earth and dies, it remains just a single grain; but if it dies, it bears much fruit" (John 12:24). The seed had been sown in the rich soil of the garden by Joseph of Arimathea and Nicodemus, sown in a new tomb that no one had used. It is about to flower. The dawn is near. Like Mary Magdalene, we shall receive more than we search for if we, too, are open to encounter the Lord.

In the garden, we see three seekers: Mary Magdalene, the Beloved Disciple, and Simon Peter. Each one searches for the Lord in their own way; each has their own way of loving and each their own emptiness. Each of these seekers has their own role in the dawning of hope. There is no rivalry. Their mutual dependence embodies the heart of synodality. All of us can identify with at least one of them. Which one are you?

Tomáš Halík has argued that the future of the Church depends on her ability to reach out to the seekers of our society. These are often the "nones." I do not mean contemplative religious sisters but the people who claim that they have no religious affiliation. They, too, are often searching for the meaning of their lives. Halík writes that Christians must thus be willing to be "seekers with those who seek and questioners with those who question."[4]

4. *Patience with God: The Story of Zacchaeus Continuing in Us*, trans. Gerard Turner (Doubleday, 2009), 9.

All the accounts of the resurrection are filled with questions. Twice Mary Magdalene is asked why she is weeping. She asks where they have put the body. They all ask why the tomb is empty. In Mark's account, the women ask, "Who will roll away the stone for us?" (16:3). Luke's accounts of the resurrection, too, are filled with questions: "Why do you look for the living among the dead?" (24:5). Jesus asks the disciples fleeing to Emmaus, "What are you discussing with each other?" (24:17). Then all of the disciples: "Why are you frightened, and why do doubts arise in your hearts?" (24:38). The resurrection bursts into our lives not as bald statement of fact but in searching questions.

Profound questions do not seek only information. They invite us to be alive in a new way and to speak in a new language. The poet Rainer Maria Rilke wrote, "Do not now seek the answers, which cannot be given you, because you would not be able to live them. And the point is, to live everything. *Live* the questions now. Perhaps you will then gradually, without noticing it, live along some distant day into the answer."[5]

The resurrection is not Jesus coming alive again after a brief interruption but a *new* way of being alive in which death has been conquered. And so it bursts into our lives in the gospels, first as urgent questions that will not let us

5. *Letters to a Young Poet*, rev. ed., trans. N. D. Herter Norton (Norton, 1954), 27.

go on living in the same way. Likewise, we come to this synod with many questions—for example, about the role of women in the Church. These are important questions. But they cannot be seen as just questions about whether something will be allowed or refused. That would be to remain the same sort of Church. The questions that we face should be more like those in the gospels, which invite us to live the risen life together more profoundly, a new Easter.

And so we must dare to bring to this synod the deepest questions in our hearts, disconcerting questions that invite us to new life. Like those three seekers in the garden, we must attend to each other's questions if we are to find a renewed way of being Church. If we have no questions, or superficial questions, our faith is dead. A certain archbishop, not present with us today, said to a group of Dominican novices, "Make sure that all of you read the *Summa* of Aquinas. It contains fifty-six thousand answers to all those who criticize the Catholic Church!"[6] Aquinas would have been horrified. As a child, legend has it, his first question was "What is God?" and his holiness was to refuse any answer for, he said, we are joined to God as to the unknown.

6. Paul Murray OP, "Dominicans and the Key of Knowledge: A Talk to Dominican Friars Studying in Rome," Pontifical University of St. Thomas Aquinas, February 19, 2023, https://angelicum.it/wp-content/uploads/2023/04/Paul-Murray-Dominicans-and-the-Key-of-Knowledge-13.Apr_.2023-vf.pdf.

If we listen to each other's questions with respect and without fear, we shall find a new way to live in the Spirit. As I said last year, the motto of the Dominican Academy in Baghdad is "Here no questions are forbidden." We are Mary Magdalene and the Beloved Disciple and Simon Peter, and it is only together that we shall find the Risen Lord who is waiting for us.

Let's look at each of these seekers and see what they can teach us about reaching out to the seekers of our time. Mary Magdalene is drawn by a love that is tender. It is down-to-earth, physical, flesh-and-blood. She wishes to care for the body of her beloved Lord. She surely stands for all those whose lives are driven by compassion for the wounded of the world: Mother Teresa, who searched for the body of her Lord on the streets of Kolkata; Saint Damien of Molokai, who gave his life to those suffering from leprosy in Hawaii.

Think also of those millions of people who do not know Christ and yet who are filled with compassion for the suffering. Like Mary Magdalene, they are searching for the bodies of the wounded. The world is filled with weeping. Four days into our last assembly, Hamas committed those terrible atrocities that plunged the Middle East into war. People are weeping in Ukraine and, yes, in Russia too, at the death and mutilation of hundreds of thousands of young people as they weep too in Sudan and Myanmar. One of the study groups convoked by the Holy Father is called Listening to the Cry of the Poor. It could be called Listening to the Cry of Those Who Weep. Mary Magdalene is their patron.

Then Mary hears her name: "Mary!" "Rabbouni!" she cries back (John 20:16). It is fitting that she whose life is driven by compassionate, tender love, should have her emptiness filled with her name. She searched for a dead body, but she found more than she could have dreamt of, the love that is alive for ever. Our God always calls us by name.

> But now thus says the Lord,
> he who created you, O Jacob,
> he who formed you, O Israel:
> Do not fear, for I have redeemed you;
> I have called you by name, you are mine. (Isa 43:1)

The calling of her name signifies an encounter, the presence of the Lord. The first thing that happens at baptism is the request for a name. "What is your name?" or "What name do you give your child?" The name is not just a label slapped on children to distinguish them from each other; that would make me Child Number 4. Our name is a sign that we are treasured by God in our uniqueness.

Pope Francis contrasted the way that the Roman emperor saw the world, through a census counting numbers, with our God: "Dear brother, dear sister, to God, who changed history in the course of a census, you are not a number; instead you are a face. . . . Christ does not look at numbers, but at faces."[7]

And so our mission, too, is to name the God who looks for us in the dark. And to treasure each other's name and face, too. We shall only mediate God's presence if we are present to each other in this synod. Gregory Boyle SJ works with young gang members in Los Angeles. The secret of his ministry is to know their names. Not just their official names or their nicknames, but the names that their mothers call them when they are not angry. When he calls young Lula by his name, he tells us, "You would have thought that I had electrocuted him. His whole body spasms with delight to be known, to be called, to hear his name uttered out loud. For his entire trip through the crosswalk, Lula kept turning back and looking at me, smiling."[8]

Tyrannical regimes erase names and faces. In Auschwitz, Saint Maximilian Kolbe became prisoner 16,670. The president of Russia has always refused to name the man who bravely opposed him, Alexei Navalny. He was just "a certain person." Similarly, Nelson Mandela became

7. "Midnight Mass: Solemnity of the Nativity of the Lord," December 24, 2023.

8. *Tattoos on the Heart: The Power of Boundless Compassion* (Free Press, 2010), 47.

the face of opposition to the apartheid regime. When he was imprisoned, it was prohibited to publish an image of his face. It was erased from the public memory. So when, after decades in prison, he was allowed to walk on the beach, no one knew him. His face had been robbed of its power.

This synod will be a moment of grace if we look at each other with compassion and see people who are like us, searching. Not representatives of parties within the Church—that horrible conservative cardinal, that frightening feminist!—but fellow searchers who are wounded and empty yet joyful, and whose names and faces we treasure. I must confess that I am terrible at remembering names, partly because I am deaf. That is my excuse. Forgive me!

But Mary Magdalene's tender love needs healing and purification. Jesus commands her, "Do not hold on to me" (John 20:17). Scholars have given some absurd explanations for this, the most implausible being that Jesus' wounds were still sore! He is saying she cannot take private possession of him. His presence is not hers to own. The resurrection is the birth of his community. "The People of God is never simply the sum of the baptised; rather, it is the 'we' of the Church" (IL 3). "But go to my brothers and say to them, 'I am ascending to my Father and your Father, to my God and your God' " (John 20:17). This is the first time in John's gospel that he calls the disciples "brothers." *Fratelli Tutti!* She must liberate her love from all exclusivity! Then she will be ready to preach the Good News to the disciples: "I have seen the Lord." This is our challenge, too. Not to cling to my English Jesus or my Dominican Jesus, but the Lord in whom we are all brothers and sisters, even the Jesuits! This synod will be fruitful if we learn to say "we." "My Father and your Father, my God and your God."

Then there is the disciple whom the Lord loved. He, too, has his way of loving and his own emptiness, the extinction of the light of his life. He lets old Peter, puffing and panting, go first into the dark tomb, but he sees the empty space between the angels and he believes. This is the love that gives sight. "*Ubi amor, ibi oculus*" (Richard of St Victor). "Where there is love, there is sight." He sees with the eyes of love and so sees love's victory. His gospel is that of the eagle, whose eyes were believed to look straight into the light of the sun and not be blinded. His search is supremely theological.

I spent two weeks this year in the École Biblique in Jerusalem. The brethren live in the shadow of death, forty minutes from Gaza. They remain there, studying the word of God, teaching and praying. They remain as a sign that "the light shines in the darkness, and the darkness did not overcome it" (John 1:5). Mary Magdalene's emptiness is healed by the calling of a name—a presence—and John's by the light that shines in an empty tomb. So he embodies all those who seek to *understand* the meaning of our lives, the God-shaped void in our hearts, as Blaise Pascal said. Christian thinkers, of course, but also everyone who struggles to find light in the darkness of our suffering: the poets and the artists and filmmakers who refuse to believe that darkness has the victory. For our preaching of the resurrection, we need them; we need to be open to their wisdom, as Saint Thomas Aquinas was to the pagan Aristotle. Aquinas wrote that "all truth, no matter by whom it is said, is from the Holy Spirit"—*omne verum, a quocumque dicatur, est a Spiritu Sancto.*[9]

Then there is Simon Peter. His emptiness is the heaviest of all, the burden of failure. He denied his friend. Surely he longs for those healing words that will be spoken at last on the beach. So our pastoral mission, too, is to be with all those who are burdened by failure and sin and share the forgiveness we have received, our own discovery of the amazing grace of the one who "saved a wretch like me. / I once was lost but now am found, / was blind but now I see." Our mission is to name the merciful one whom we, too, need, as Peter did.

So in this first resurrection scene, we see how the Lord responds to three forms of searching, corresponding to three voids in our lives: tender love that searches for pres-

9. *ST* I–II, q. 109, a. 1, ad. 1.

ence, for meaning and light, and for forgiveness. Each searcher needs the other. Without Mary Magdalene, they would not have come to the tomb; she declares that the Lord is present. Without the Beloved Disciple, they would not have understood the emptiness of the tomb as the victory of the resurrection. Without Peter, they would not have understood that resurrection is the triumph of mercy.

Each represents a group that felt in some way excluded at the last assembly. Mary Magdalene also reminds us of how women are often excluded from formal positions of authority in the Church. How are we to find a way forward, which justice and our faith demand? Their search is ours. At the last assembly, many theologians also felt marginal. Some wondered why they had bothered to come. We cannot get anywhere without them. And the group that was most resistant to the synodal path was the pastors, the parish priests who especially share Peter's role as shepherds of mercy. The Church cannot become truly synodal without them, too.

When nearly everyone feels that *they* are the excluded ones, there should be no competition for victimhood! The search in the dark for the Lord needs all of these witnesses, as the synod needs all of the ways that we love and search for the Lord, as we need the seekers of our time, even if they do not share our faith.

How is this to overflow into mission? These words are attributed, somewhat inaccurately, to Antoine de

Saint-Exupéry: "If you wish to construct a boat, do not gather your men and women to give them orders, or to explain each detail of what they must do or where to find everything. Instead, give birth in the hearts of your men and women the desire for the sea."[10] Give people a taste of the infinite, and they will find their own ways to make boats and set off into the vast ocean.

Each of these witnesses of the resurrection is touched by a love which is infinite. Mary Magdalene is touched by an infinite tenderness; the Beloved Disciple is moved by the search for boundless meaning; Peter, by the need for the mercy that is without limits, forgiving not seven times but seventy times seven times. If we open ourselves to each other's infinite yearning, we shall launch the boat of mission. Only together shall we, in the words of Ephesians, "have the power to comprehend, with all the saints, what is the breadth and length and height and depth, and to know the love of Christ that surpasses knowledge, so that you may be filled with all the fullness of God" (3:18-19).

We may feel we are in dark, but the Lord is here. Let us search for him together.

10. These lines, in fact, seem to be a recently constructed paraphrase of a passage from Saint-Exupéry's 1948 book *Citadelle* (published in English as *The Wisdom of the Sands*).

In the next session, we shall find the disciples once again in the dark, in the locked room. We shall also meet another searcher, Thomas.

The Locked Room

John 20:19-29

This morning we saw the disciples running around in the dark, searching for the Lord. The Beloved Disciple sees and believes. It is dawn. Now it is evening, we are back in the dark, and they are immobilized in the locked room.

The morning was dark at first, because they had not yet found the Risen Lord. The evening is dark because they are not yet filled with the Holy Spirit, the living breath of the Risen Lord. The stone has been rolled away and Jesus has burst out of the empty tomb. They are still in the tomb of the locked room. Genesis says that in the beginning, "The LORD God formed man from the dust of the ground, and breathed into his nostrils the breath of life; and the man became a living being" (2:7). Now Jesus gives them the breath of eternal life: "Receive the Holy Spirit. If you forgive the sins of any, they are forgiven them; if you retain the sins of any, they are retained" (John 20:22-23). They share in his risen life, and so they are ready to be sent to preach.

This morning we saw that the mission of the synodal Church calls us to be like Mary Magdalene, the Beloved Disciple, and Peter, searchers for the Risen Lord. We, too, must be close to the searchers of our time. But we shall only become *preachers* of the resurrection if we are alive in God. No one will believe a zombie. Remember the words of Saint Irenaeus: *Gloria Dei homo vivens*—the glory of God is a human being fully alive. Like Lazarus, we hear the voice of the Lord summoning us out of our locked rooms: "Come out and live."

Holiness is being alive in God. A cousin of Charles de Foucauld, who was much given to the pleasures of eating and drinking, described a visit from Charles, who had returned to Paris for a short visit after years of living in the Sahara: "He entered the room and peace entered with him. The glow of his eyes and especially that very humble smile had taken over his whole person. . . . There was an incredible joy emanating from him. . . . I, upon seeing that my whole sum of satisfactions did not weigh more than a tiny fraction in comparison with the complete happiness of the ascetic, found rising within me a strange feeling not of envy but of respect."[1] It has

1. Fergus Fleming, *The Sword and the Cross* (Granta, 2003), 235-36.

been said of Saint Teresa of Avila that she had "the rapturous consciousness of life beyond self."[2] Or think of Carlo Acutis, a handsome Italian teenager who played video games. Millennials can see here one of their own generation who is truly alive. So the challenge for us is to help each other to breathe deeply the rejuvenating Holy Spirit and live! A bit of a challenge for me now in my eightieth year!

The first task of leadership is to lead the flock out of the tiny sheepfolds into the fresh air of the Holy Spirit. Leadership opens the locked doors of stuffy rooms. The disciples are imprisoned by fear. So let us think of the fears that may prevent us from becoming alive in God and so preachers of the gospel of abundant life.

We all know the fear of being hurt. Some of us come to this assembly fearful we shall not find recognition and acceptance. Our treasured hopes for the Church may be scorned. We may feel invisible. Do we dare to speak and risk rejection? If you are not used to this world of the Vatican, with its grandiose titles and strange clothes, it can be intimidating. We dare to take the risk of getting hurt, because the Risen Lord, too, is wounded. He shows them his hands and his side. We should not be afraid of getting hurt.

2. George Eliot, *Middlemarch* (Prelude) (Penguin, 2015; orig. 1871-72), 3.

The Easter Preface goes further: he lives forever slain ("*sed semper vivit occisus*").[3] Remember those words of my brother Herbert McCabe: "If you love, you will be hurt and even killed. If you do not love, you are dead already." Becoming alive in God means being unafraid of wounds.

Our priory in Jerusalem is situated near the Damascus Gate. This is a tense place where the Old City opens onto the Arab quarter. A group of young Jews stood there, blindfolded, offering "free hugs" to anyone who wanted one. They took the risk that instead of a hug they might receive a knife.

Alan Paton was a South African novelist who courageously campaigned against apartheid. In one of his novels, one of his characters says, "When I go up there, which is my intention, the Big Judge will say to me, Where are your wounds? and if I say I haven't any, he will say, Was there nothing to fight for?"[4]

In the Philippines I met a woman who was scarred by leprosy. For most of her life she lived in a leprosarium run by a branch of the Dominican Order, the Brothers of Saint Martin. Many of them suffer from leprosy, too. She was afraid to leave the place, even when she was

3. Preface III of Easter: "the Lamb, once slain, who lives for ever." *The Roman Missal* (Liturgical Press, 2011), 562.

4. *Ah, But your Land is Beautiful* (Scribner, 1981), 66–67.

cured. People would see her scars and be afraid, and so she remained trapped inside. And one day she dared to venture outside, and she discovered a new mission: to travel all over Asia, inviting people who suffered from leprosy to come out and live.

We can embrace the risk of being hurt because the Lord has given us his peace. The film *Of Gods and Men* tells the story of the Trappist monks who refused to flee Algeria when terrorist violence broke out in the 1990s. Frère Luc, the ancient doctor of the community, says, "I'm not scared of death. I'm a free man."[5] In the old Dominican Rite of the Mass, the priest kissed the chalice of Christ's shed blood before he offered the greeting of peace.

The first creation began with "Let there be light." The new creation begins with "Let there be peace." These words cannot be unspoken. Mahatma Gandhi had a picture of Jesus in his room with the quotation from Ephesians, "He is our peace" (2:14). Jesus *is* God's Sabbath. In the early Church, "*in pace*" was written on Christian tombs. We are baptized into Christ's peace, which nothing can destroy. We should not be ruled by fear.

In the late sixties, my Dominican community in Oxford was attacked by a crazy group. Not the Jesuits! At two a.m., two small bombs blew out all the windows in

5. *Of Gods and Men* (*Des hommes et des dieux*), directed by Xavier Beauvois (Why Not Productions, 2010).

the front of the priory. We were all awoken and rushed down. The police and the ambulances came. The prior alone, Fergus Kerr, was still fast asleep. The youngest novice was sent to his room. "Fergus, Fergus, wake up. There has been a bomb attack." "Anybody dead?" "No." "Anyone wounded?" "No." "Go away and let me sleep. We will think about it in the morning." My first lesson in leadership.

The victory is won. When his executioners came for Dietrich Bonhoeffer, his last message was for his friend Bishop Bell of Chichester. It was: "Tell the bishop, our victory is certain."[6] One of the brethren may have a sex change; the bursar may run away with the money; the church may be blown up! But Christ has died, Christ is risen, and Christ will come again.

God's peace does not mean that we *feel* at peace. My fellow novice Simon Tugwell OP wrote, "It is not a subjective sensation of peace that is required; if we are in Christ, we can be in peace (*in pace*) and therefore unflustered even when we feel no peace."[7] Perhaps for many of us, the most profound challenge is to be at peace with ourselves. Do we dare to look at our own troubled and

6. See Dietrich Bonhoeffer, *Works*, vol. 16: *Conspiracy and Imprisonment: 1940–1945* (Fortress, 2006), 468–69.

7. *Reflections on the Beatitudes: Soundings in Christian Traditions* (Darton, Longman and Todd, 1980), 114.

divided hearts, the bits of ourselves that we do not like? The temptation is to project onto others what we fear and dislike in ourselves. Tugwell again: "Peace comes with an unflustered self-knowledge. . . . The way to peace is the acceptance of truth. Any bit of us that we refuse to accept will be our enemy, forcing us into defensive postures. And the discarded pieces of ourselves will rapidly find incarnation in those around us."[8] When people passionately denounce others, one wonders what they fear about themselves!

Our fierce love of the Church can also, paradoxically, make us narrow-minded, fearful that it will be harmed by destructive reforms that undermine the traditions we love or the fear that it will not become the wide-open home for which we long. It is deeply sad that often the Church is wounded by those who also love the Church, but differently! Saint Ephraim said that the Catholic Church is "the big church with the big lap."[9] I met a German Lutheran theologian who taught at Oxford, and he said, "I am afraid that Catholics are becoming Protestant." Sometimes we forget the wideness of Catholicism, with its both/and. The truth we love is, as Bishop Robert Barron wrote, "as wide the universe and as specific as the

8. *Reflections on the Beatitudes*, 112.

9. Quoted in Simon Tugwell, "Scholarship, Sanctity and Spirituality," *Communio* 11, no. 1 (Spring 1984): 46–59, at 53.

person of Jesus."[10] Perfect love drives out fear. Let it drive out the fear of those whose visions of the Church are different. The Church is in the hands of the Lord, and God has promised that the powers of death shall not prevail against it (see Matt 16:18).

During the Napoleonic era, a flustered monsignor came anxiously to see the Vatican's secretary of state, Cardinal Consalvi, and said, "Your Eminence, the situation is very serious. Napoleon wishes to destroy the church." To which the cardinal replied, "Not even we have succeeded in doing that!"

Our very love of the Church, in utterly different ways, can lock us inside a narrow world, gazing at our ecclesiastical navels, watching others, ready to spot their deviations and denounce them, as the Pharisees watched Jesus to condemn him. Pope Francis, before his election, said that the Lord would come knocking on the door and demand to be let out of the sacristy! Of course, there are changes for which some of us long, but let that not lock us inside our little churchy world. We shall be boring! God is revealed on mountaintops with unbounded horizons and outside the camp.

Our liberation from these small rooms demands not just courage but God's healing forgiveness. The Risen

10. Quoted by Michael Heher, *The Lost Art of Walking on Water: Reimagining the Priesthood* (Paulist, 2003), 132.

Lord says, "If you forgive the sins of any, they are forgiven them; if you retain the sins of any, they are retained" (John 20:23).

Sin locks us inside prisons of narcissism and party politics, like the elder son who sulks and will not join in the party to welcome home his prodigal brother. Herbert McCabe again:

> Our very nature calls us to something new and frightening. . . . We are the kind of being that finds its fulfilment, its happiness and flourishing only in giving itself up, and getting beyond itself. We need to lose our selves in love; that is what we fear. We are summoned to venture into what is unknown, to abandon what is familiar and safe, and set out on a journey or quest. And yet we do not like to take risks. We settle for the person that we have achieved or constructed because we are afraid of being made in the image of God. This failure to respond to the summons into life, this failure of faith, is called sin.[11]

Sin is the refusal to say yes to life.

So this synod is not a place for negotiating structural change but for choosing life, for conversion and forgiveness. The Lord summons us out of the small places in

11. *God Matters* (Continuum, 1987), 94–95.

which we have taken refuge and in which we have imprisoned others. The hymn composed by Frederick Faber, the nineteenth-century Oratorian, proclaims, "There is a wideness in God's mercy, / like the wideness of the sea."

Let us pray that Christ's peace will melt the violence that dwells in our hearts and that crucified Our Lord. Dorothy Day asserted that "the big fight is against violence more than it is against atheism."[12] She said, "Christians, when they are seeking to defend their faith by arms, by force and violence, are like those who said to Our Lord, 'Come down from the Cross. If you are the Son of God, save Yourself.' "[13] So in this synod, let us overcome all the violence in our hearts—violent thoughts and violent words. Our global culture cultivates a violent imagination. "By the age of 18, American teenagers will on average have witnessed on the media 200,000 acts of violence and 16,000 murders. Often these are glamorised or treated as humorous. Violence is normalised and even seems harmless as one zaps demonic enemies in a video game. This seemingly innocent entertainment nurtures a violent imagination which has no guilt in destruction because [in the cyber world,] nothing is real."[14]

12. *The Duty of Delight: The Diaries of Dorothy Day*, ed. Robert Ellsberg (Marquette University Press, 2008), 25.

13. *The Duty of Delight*, 22.

14. Timothy Radcliffe, *Alive in God: A Christian Imagination* (Bloomsbury Continuum, 2019), 196. The data is from *Children, Violence and*

The Body of Christ is disfigured by poisonous websites, filled with cruel accusation, caricature, and hatred. Anyone who exercises any form of leadership in the Church will have experienced this. I was accused as master of the Order of having given permission to a provincial to live with his mistress, a nun, in a railway carriage!

The Holy Spirit breathes within us. Our violent world deprives so many of even the breath of life. The sin of racism, for example, literally stops people from breathing. "I can't breathe" were the last words of an African American, Eric Garner, repeated eleven times and recorded on the phones of onlookers while he was choked to death by the police on Staten Island, New York, ten years ago. These words have become the rallying cry of African Americans, symbolic of their oppression. They were also the last words of Jamal Khashoggi, the Saudi journalist who was murdered in his country's consulate in Turkey on October 2, 2018. Let us give each other breathing space, the oxygen of debate.

This indestructible peace does not mean that we live in perfect harmony. We are gathered in this assembly because we do not. But no discord can destroy our peace in Christ, for we are one in Him. Thomas Merton wrote in his Asian journal, "We are already one. But we imagine that we are not. And what we have to recover is our

---

the Media: A Report for Parents and Policy Makers (Senate Committee on the Judiciary, September 14, 1999).

original unity. What we have to be is what we are."[15] In this synod, we must be what we are most deeply.

But Thomas was out when Jesus appeared. Perhaps because *he* was unafraid? When Lazarus was ill, he declared that he was willing to go up to Jerusalem and die with Jesus (see John 11:16). He is passionate about the truth: "I will never, ever, ever believe unless I put my fingers in his wounds" (see John 20:25).[16] And when he sees the Lord, he makes his passionate confession: "My Lord and my God." This passionate disciple also invites us out of the small room.

"My Lord and my God." This is literally a theological statement: a word about God. The theme of this assembly is how to be a synodal Church on mission. The heart of this mission is to teach our doctrinal truths. When Mary Magdalene is called by name, she replies, "Rabbouni," Teacher. In the last words of Matthew's gospel, Jesus sends his disciples out to teach all the nations. How are we to share our Christian teachings with a world hungry for meaning?

15. *The Asian Journal of Thomas Merton*, ed. Naomi Burton, Brother Patrick Hart, and James Laughlin (New Directions, 1973), 308.

16. See Timothy L. Fox, "Jesus' Resurrection Appearances," Modern Reformation, November 1, 2019, https://www.modernreformation.org/resources/essays/jesus-resurrection-appearances. Fox points out that in John 20:25, the gospel writer has Thomas use a double negative, "plus [an] aorist subjunctive (denying that something is even possible). . . . Unlike in English, in Greek a double negative emphasizes the denial."

In the poor suburbs of Paris, young Catholics are asking to be taught the doctrines of the Church so that they can talk to their Muslim friends about what the Church teaches. There was a gathering earlier this year called *Assume ta foi en banlieue*—"Embrace Your Faith in the Suburbs."[17] The young are hungry for the rich meat of the Church's teaching: "My Lord and my God." They will not be satisfied if we just offer them a Jesus who was a nice guy and who wants us to be kind to each other.

Our society is afflicted by a profound prejudice against dogma. Steve Jobs, co-founder of Apple, summed this up in his commencement speech at Stanford in 2005: "Your time is limited, so don't waste it living someone else's life. Don't be trapped by dogma—which is living with the results of other people's thinking."[18] He was, of course, merely repeating a stale dogma of our times and *not* thinking for himself.

G. K. Chesterton asserted, "There are only two kinds of people, those who accept dogmas and know it, and those who accept dogmas and don't know it. . . . Trees

17. See Arnaud Bevilaqua, "The 'Great Awakening' of Young Catholics on the Outskirts of Paris," *La Croix International*, March 22, 2024, https://international.la-croix.com/religion/the-great-awakening-of-young-catholics-on-the-outskirts-of-paris.

18. " 'You've Got to Find What You Love,' Jobs Says," *Stanford Report*, June 12, 2005, https://news.stanford.edu/stories/2005/06/youve-got-find-love-jobs-says.

have no dogmas. Turnips are singularly broadminded."[19] Some dogmas of our time are indeed stuffy locked rooms without oxygen: relativism; all sorts of fundamentalism, materialistic, nationalistic; scientism; religious fundamentalism. They lock people in small, fearful imaginations.

But the great teachings of our faith, our Creed in essence, unlock the doors of our hearts and minds. They push us beyond small answers and propel us on the endless search for the one who is infinite love and the truth, who forever exceeds our grasp. When I was a young friar in the late sixties, and everything seemed to be falling apart, we remained in the Order because we glimpsed the radiant beauty of the Creed, the truth we do not possess but which possesses us. The young will be satisfied with nothing less.

How can we invite the people of our time to enter into the wide-open space of our faith? How, for example, can we touch their imagination with the glorious doctrine of the Trinity, the most down-to-earth and practical teaching there is? We choose ten times a day for or against the love that is Trinitarian, equal and forever. For this we need the help of theologians.

Yes, theologians sometimes retreat into the locked room of academia for fear of conversation with the people

19. "The Mercy of Mr. Arnold Bennett," in *Fancies Versus Fads* (Dodd, Mead, 1923), http://www.gkc.org.uk/gkc/books/Fancies_Versis_Fads.txt.

of God. When I studied in Paris as a young brother, I asked another Dominican what his doctorate was on. He replied, "My young brother"—he was just a year older than I was—"I will not try to explain. You would not understand." Twenty years later, when I returned on visitation as master of the Order, I saw him and said nothing!

Of course, we need academic theologians—exegetes and philologists and historians—who keep us in what Saint Paul calls "the obedience of faith" (Rom 1:5). Otherwise, we shall use the Scriptures for our own purposes and not God's. But this tough discipline of study is ultimately at the service of conversation with our contemporaries, to accompany them on the journey into the infinite mystery of the divine love. We need theologians to help our conversation with each other at this synod!

The day after the last assembly, Pope Francis called for a theology that is in charitable conversation with people of other convictions. He quoted words he had written to the students of the Catholic University of Argentina: "Do not settle for a desktop theology. Your place for reflection is the frontier. . . . Even good theologians, like good shepherds, have the odour of the people and of the street and, by their reflection, pour oil and wine onto the wounds of mankind."[20] Good theology opens the doors

20. *Motu proprio Ad Theologiam Promovendam*, November 1, 2023, quoting "Letter of His Holiness Pope Francis to the Grand Chancellor of

of stuffy rooms. Like Thomas the Apostle, it is passionate and unafraid. It embraces new ways of speaking new languages. A synodal Church on mission dares to teach boldly and humbly.

the 'Pontificia Universidad Católica Argentina' for the 100th Anniversary of the Founding of the Faculty of Theology," March 3, 2015.

The Stranger on the Beach

John 21:1-14

"That *night* they caught nothing" (John 21:3, emphasis mine). Every one of these resurrection appearances begins in the dark. For Mary Magdalene, it was the dark of her ignorance of the resurrection. But he is there waiting for her. For the disciples in the locked room, it was the darkness of their fear. Christ rose from the dead on Easter Sunday, conquering the night, and yet time and again we find ourselves back in the dark, today especially the darkness of war. We think especially of our brothers and sisters in Lebanon, some of whom have courageously made the journey to be with us at the synod; the darkness of the crisis of sexual abuse, and so on.

What is the night enveloping these disciples who have gone fishing? We are back in the ordinary world. Peter says, "I am going fishing." They are back to the old routine. It is almost as if nothing had happened in Jerusalem. Their nets are empty. They are empty. The stranger asks if they have even a tiny bit to eat. They all answer together, "No." In Greek, *ou*. The word is as empty as they are. *Ou!* The fishers of human beings can't even catch the smallest fish.

We have all known those moments when we seem to achieve nothing. Some of us have come to this assembly with hope and excitement, thanks be to God. For others, the initial enthusiasm has faded. Those who began with enthusiasm and excitement might be wondering whether we are going anywhere. Some of us never believed we were anyway. *Ou!* The most common question I have received about the synod these last eleven months has been skeptical: Has anything been achieved? Isn't it all a waste of time and money? *Ou!*

But the stranger is there on the beach even before they spot him. God is always there first, before we notice. In the Prologue of the Rule of Saint Benedict, God says, "My eyes will be upon you and my ears will listen for your prayers; and even before you ask me, I will say to you, Here I am."[1] God is there, waiting, even before we pray.

1. *RB 1980: The Rule of St. Benedict*, trans. Timothy Fry OSB (Liturgical Press, 1981), Prologue.

Why don't they recognize him? You might think this is one of those obscure questions about which scholars like to write incomprehensible articles, but it is profoundly relevant to us in this synod. How are we to recognize the Lord who is with us today but whom we may not have recognized?

It is not that he *looks* different. No, it is because they had never *really* seen him before. Herbert McCabe OP puts it well: "People are not just recognizing Jesus as the man they knew was killed. They are recognizing him as the man they *sort* of knew and *thought* they knew, but didn't *really* know until now."[2] He *is* the mystery of Love Incarnate, and they are only now beginning to glimpse the height and depth of love that surpasses all understanding. It is the Beloved Disciple who says, "It is the Lord" because he has loving eyes. Early theologians often asked why Jesus did not appear to his enemies, like Pontius Pilate. He could have jumped up and down in front of Pilate, and still Pilate would not have seen him.

Love "is a growing word, one whose meaning changes and develops."[3] As children, we think that our mother's love consists in providing us food when we demand it and never leaving us alone. As we grow up, we come to

2. *God, Christ and Us*, ed. Brian Davies OP (Continuum, 2005), 94.

3. Herbert McCabe OP, *Law, Love and Language* (Continuum, 2003), 18.

understand that sometimes love demands being absent or refusing to give you what you want, such as an iPhone.

In 2012, a French Dominican called Jean-Joseph Lataste was beatified. (Or as the BBC put it, "beautified"!) His life was turned upside down when, in 1864, he visited a prison for women. Most of them had been prostitutes or had committed infanticide. He looked at them and said, "My sisters." He founded a congregation of sisters in which they could live along with other women. Many pious, bourgeois people were disgusted. They had not yet learned to *see* love in action. They did not recognize the stranger on the beach.

Biblical scholars spend hours in silence in libraries studying obscure, dead languages. This looks, to some, to be a waste of time, but it, too, is an act of love. We do not gather in synod to negotiate compromises or bash opponents. We are here to learn from each other what is the meaning of this odd word *love*. Every one of us is a beloved disciple who has a particular gift for seeing the stranger on the beach and saying, "It is the Lord."

The turning point for the apostles in this story is when they obey the voice of the Lord and cast the net on the other side. It seems pointless. They are the ones who know about fishing. Why obey this stranger who knows nothing about fishing? We, too, have come to this synod in obedience. For many it seems pointless. We have labored days and nights and perhaps doubt that anything will be achieved. But the Church says, "Come," and we have come, or nearly all of us. We have cast the net on the other side of the boat even when some of us think that there will be no catch. But this obedience will be fruitful in ways that we do not imagine.

Here we come to the great puzzle: 153 fat fish. I could bore you for hours with all the marvelous and often absurd explanations of this number. Why 153? Some say there must have been 153 of them. But imagine counting all those fish, leaping all over the place. Others refer to the 153 churches that may have existed at the time. Still others to the 153 nations that were then known. It clearly means abundance. God's abundant providence is at work. Saint John Henry Newman described providence as "God's noiseless work." Our *Instrumentum Laboris* opens with a quotation from Isaiah:

> On this mountain the Lord of the universe will
> make for all peoples
> a feast of rich food, a feast of well-aged wines,
> of rich food filled with marrow, of well-aged wines
> strained clear.
> (IL, Introduction; Isa 25:6)

The Kingdom bursts into our lives with conviviality, with excess, like all of that wine at Cana. Saint Dominic came back to the monastery of nuns in Rome late at night after a preaching mission. He woke up the nuns so that he could tell them about his preaching. He asked for wine. There was only a little left. The nuns brought a cup, which he passed around, saying to the sisters, "*Bibite satis*"—drink up, drink enough. And the cup never ran out.

We must dare to trust that the divine providence will bless this synod abundantly, "good measure, pressed down, shaken together, running over, will be put into your lap" (Luke 6:38). We are not here for a meager meal but for the *haute cuisine* of the Kingdom, if we desire it enough. Not *la nouvelle cuisine*, for which you need your glasses even to see it!

Peter is transformed instantly. At the beginning of this scene, he is empty. He has fallen back into his old life. It is as if nothing has happened. Now he stands up and puts on his clothes before jumping into the sea (see John 21:7). We usually take our clothes off when we go swimming, but this is a sign of his dignity restored, just as the father clothes his prodigal son when he comes home. Despite his shame of the Lord, he swims toward his friend. I would have been so ashamed that I would have swum in the opposite direction. The other disciples struggle to haul ashore the catch. Peter does so single-handed. What is Peter's secret? Whatever he has done, he returns to the Lord time and again. His love is stronger than his shame.

Jesus said, "I, when I am lifted up from the earth, will draw all people to myself" (John 12:32). Now we see Peter drawing—it is the same word in Greek—the net full of fat fish by himself, and the net is not broken. This is not due to his strength but his cooperation with the attraction of the Lord, the magnetic pull of the Risen Lord. It is the Lord's attractiveness that pulls the unbroken net ashore. The Petrine ministry of unity is not about policing God's wayward children. It is about revealing the attractiveness of the Lord, who draws us together. We are drawn by the beauty of the cross.

When I came to the synod last year, I thought the great challenge was to overcome the poisonous opposition between so-called traditionalists and progressives. How can we heal that polarization that is so alien to Catholicism? But as I listened, there seemed to be an even more fundamental challenge: How can the Church embrace all of the diverse cultures of our world? How can we haul in the 450 members of the synod without the net breaking?

When the Berlin Wall fell in 1989, the Cold War was deemed to be over. Francis Fukuyama published a book called *The End of History and the Last Man*,[4] arguing that we had entered a new era, the triumph of Western liberal democracy. Every nation seemed destined to "evolve" into our Western way of life. Some countries, especially in the global South, just had to catch up. This was an

4. Free Press, 1992.

illusion from which the West is slowly waking up. Instead, we live in a multipolar world in which many from the global South see the West as decadent and doomed. We live in a post-Western world.[5] Many Westerners do not yet realize this.

We await a new Pentecost, in which each culture speaks in its own native tongue and is understood. This is also our task during the synod and the foundation of our mission to our torn and divided world. We ask for the prayers of Mary, untier of knots, and Peter, the mender of nets!

First of all, let us recognize that we need each other if we are to be Catholic. The diverse cultures gathered in this assembly offer healing to each other, challenge each other's prejudices, and summon each other to a deeper understanding of love. Every culture has its own way of seeing the stranger on the beach and saying, "It is the Lord."

For example, Pope Benedict XVI confessed that the West is suffering from "a form of sickness of the spirit,"[6] what Saint John Paul II called a "culture of death." Either we flee from death and pretend it will never happen, or

5. See Oliver Stuenkel, *Post-Western World: How Emerging Powers Are Remaking Global Order* (Polity, 2016).

6. Homily at the opening of the Second Special Assembly for Africa of the Synod Bishops, October 4, 2009.

we seek to master it with assisted dying. Like Peter, we Westerners need help to see the Risen Lord on the shore who has triumphed over death. We need help to live aware of our mortality in hope.

A beloved French Dominican died during a general chapter in Bogota. The brethren from the West were overcome with grief. A young Colombian brother protested, "This is not the time of death. This is the time of faith."[7] Our brother in this synod, Father Orobator SJ, gave thanks that he was raised by parents who practiced traditional African religion, with its profound sense of the gift of life. He wrote, "Central to the whole religious system throughout Africa is a *deep belief in the livingness of creation*."[8] You do not know what it means to live if you hide from death. We have much to learn from our brothers and sisters in other parts of the globe, whose eyes are open to death and so understand more of what it means to be alive in the Risen Lord.

Perhaps our greatest challenge is to embrace what Pope Benedict called "interculturality." This is not the time for a theoretical exploration of what this means. Instead, let us imagine a net. A net consists of empty holes

7. I was reminded of this incident by Frère Bruno Cadoret OP, master of the Order.

8. Agbonkhianmeghe E. Orobator, *Religion and Faith in Africa: Confessions of an Animist* (Orbis, 2018), 16.

linked together by ropes. Spaces and bonds. Without both, there would be no net to haul in the fish.

When cultures meet, we should treasure the space between them. Neither should devour the other, as is happening with the globalization of consumerism. We should reverence cultural difference. Remember that marvelous German word, *zwischenraum*, "the space in between." This is the fertile space between cultures when each retains its identity but is open to the other. Aquinas said that when there is love, the two become one but remain distinct.[9]

No single culture could ever bind us together—not Latin, not even Thomism! The net is untorn because every culture is open in its own way to the truth. Cardinal Ratzinger explained in a talk, given in Hong Kong in 1992, that "the fundamental openness of each person to the other can only be explained by the hidden fact that our souls have been touched by truth; and this explains the essential agreement which exists even between cultures most removed from each other. . . . No one grasps the whole; the myriad insights form and build a kind of mosaic displaying their complementarity and interrelatedness. In order to be whole, everybody needs each other. Human beings approach the unity and wholeness of our being only in the reciprocity of all great cultural

9. *ST* II–II, q. 17, art. 3.

achievements."[10] Our interculturality is the great gift of Catholicism to a world that is fragmenting.

We are bound together by our shared faith, the Creed, which transcends any culture. But how can one translate *homoousios* into Swahili, Hindi, or Japanese? Surely the net needs to be held together also by mutual delight, friendship, shared joy, and even laughter. One of the most fascinating examples of this interculturality was the Jesuit mission to China in the sixteenth century. This encounter of West and East flourished through a friendship that was mutually enriching. In fact, Matteo Ricci's first book was on friendship. Friendship knit the net.

But rather than talk about these admirable Jesuits, I shall glance humbly at two examples I have experienced in my own Order, just to help us imagine our task in the synod. One of my favorite places is a farm in Benin, founded by our brother Godfrey Nzamujo OP. It is called Songhai, after the great African empire that flourished in the region five hundred years ago. Nzamujo learned to farm at home in Africa and studied Western science in California. Songhai is the fruit of African and Western farming. The farm began as one hectare of wasteland that no one wanted and now covers twenty-four hectares

10. "Christ, Faith and the Challenge of Cultures," Meeting with the Doctrinal Commissions in Asia, Hong Kong, March 3, 1993, https://www.vatican.va/roman_curia/congregations/cfaith/incontri/rc_con_cfaith_19930303_hong-kong-ratzinger_en.html.

and educates young farmers from all over Africa and, indeed, the world.

Nothing is wasted here. Flies fatten on the leftovers of the restaurant and then are fed to the fish. Nzamujo calls Songhai the Sheraton Hotel for flies. All the animals and plants thrive in mutual dependence. At Songhai, even the mosquitoes have their role to play in the balance of life, even though they are not one of God's best ideas!

The Eucharist here is seen within an ecology of gratitude. Nzamujo said, "The Mass is the combination of the gifts of the sun, the water, and the soil. The wine is the pain and anguish coming from the grapes that have to be crushed, but it becomes a symbol of friendship." Songhai radiates hope. He said, "There is a time to be born and a time to die, because that is nature. Africa may seem to be on the losing side, but honestly, from what I feel, from what I see, tomorrow is African time."

This is what happens when cultures meet in friendship and beget hope. The space between us is bridged by mutual delight and even laughter. Nzamujo maintains that his pigs symbolized both the project and our friendship, since they are the result of interbreeding between big white Yorkshire pigs like me and small black African pigs like him. Difference is fertile. It knits the net.

Another brief example: A Japanese Dominican, Shigeto Oshida (1922–2003), described himself as a Buddhist who met Jesus. He founded an ashram near Mount Fuji, where Christians and Buddhists lived together in harmony. He detested the tendency of the West to eviscerate reality with abstract notions. He called this "the third leg of the chicken," which was neither the right leg nor the left leg but an abstract nonexistent leg. He said, "We Japanese know in our blood what religion is. The Catholic Church is not a box of chocolates or a business."[11]

When Oshida gave retreats, especially for bishops used to the sedentary life, he enjoyed sending them to plant rice in the paddy fields, impervious to their protests about backaches. He wrote, "A farmer who works hard from dawn to dusk knows that a grain of rice is not his product, a thing made by his own effort, but something given to him by God. He must offer the grain of rice to God who is hidden but who gives everything. He must say 'This is yours.'"[12]

Oshida was deeply critical of Western culture, but, like Nzamujo, he reached across cultural divisions with laughter and delight. He liked to joke that God tricked him into becoming a Christian and then a Dominican because he met wonderful Christians and then Dominicans and thought we were all like that. He would laugh, saying, "I was wrong! God cheated me."

11. Lucien Miller, *Jesus in the Hands of Buddha: The Life and Legacy of Shigeto Vincent Oshida, OP* (Liturgical Press, 2023), 135.

12. Shigeto Oshida, *Takemori Sōan: Teachings of Shigeto Oshida, a Zen Master*, ed. Claudia Mattiello (Talleres Gráficos Color Efe, 2007).

So Peter's net is filled with space and held together by truth, delight, and joy. It is hauled to the beach not by juridical power but by the attractiveness of the Lord who, when he is lifted up, draws all to himself. Beauty hauls the net to the shore. Think of Matatoshi Asari (b. 1931), a Japanese Catholic from Nagasaki, who sent cherry trees, symbols of reconciliation, to all the nations that had been harmed by the Second World War.[13]

May God bless this synod with such loving cultural encounters, in which the two become one but remain distinct. No culture can dominate. But we need to be acutely aware of how power imbalance is at play in our conversations. The encounter of cultures is never innocent or merely cerebral. Colonialism still structures our world. Father Orobator shares an African proverb: "Until the lion learns to speak and write, the tale of the hunt will always glorify the hunter."[14] The lion does now speak, but the West does not listen.

According to a song from my youth, "Money makes the world go around." We may live in a post-Western world, but the banking system is still controlled by the West. Imperialism is not over. Western institutions and

13. See Naoko Abe, *The Martyr and the Red Kimono: A Fearless Priest's Sacrifice and a New Generation of Hope in Japan* (Chatto and Windus, 2024).

14. *Religion and Faith in Africa*, xviii.

governments are the tax collectors of the world. But the stranger on the beach was not a member of the wealthy elite. He was crucified by the greatest imperial power of his day, a death reserved for slaves, intended to humiliate. So let us listen with acute attention to those who are crucified today by the imperial powers of our time. Let us listen with humility to each other. It is a humble Simon Peter whom we shall meet in the next session.

Breakfast with the Lord

John 21:15-25

Now at last, for the first time since his denial, Jesus and Simon Peter talk to each other. It is not clear whether it is the fish being grilled or Peter! Jesus asks Peter, "Do you love me?" There is not a word about his denial. What matters is not then but *now*, today. Łukasz Popko OP, of the École Biblique, has written, "Note that Jesus did not ask about the past. He did not ask for an explanation or excuse. Secondly, he did not ask about the future: Will you love me? He did not ask for a promise: Promise that you will love me. He asked about the present! So often we avoid the question of love and the corresponding answer because we are stuck with the failures of the past or in the fantasies of the future."[1]

1. Personal communication.

The Divine Office begins every day with God's plea to us: "Oh that *today* you would listen to my voice." Today is the only day that exists; God's present is the present. Today during this synod, we must hearken to the Lord and each other. We cannot delay. If we do listen, today will be a new beginning. Shortly before he died, Cardinal Martini surprised his friend Damiano Modena when he suddenly said, "Il cristianesimo è solo all'inizio"—Christianity is only at the beginning.

Why do we delay? Skepticism and inertia hold us back. My Irish brethren joke that the Irish language has thirty-two words for *tomorrow*, but none of them have the same sense of urgency as *mañana*! When Peter saw the Lord on the beach, he did not hesitate to throw himself into the water and swim for the land. *Carpe diem*. Seize the day!

The conversation at breakfast is perhaps the most subtle and delicate in the Bible. The shame of Peter's denial at another charcoal fire is in the air, but nothing is said explicitly. With gentleness and perhaps even a smile, Jesus opens the space for Peter to unsay three times his threefold denial. Do we rub people's noses in the folly of what they have said or done? Or do we gently open a healing space for them to move on?

"Do you love me more than these?" (John 21:15). In Matthew and Mark, which John surely knew, Peter had claimed exactly that on his night of shame. "Even though all become deserters, I will not" (Mark 14:29). I love you best! And now, he does it again! There is a lot of debate about the meanings of the different words for *love* here, *agape* and *philia*. I am convinced that Peter claims that not only does he love Jesus, but he loves him with the best of all loves, *philia*, friendship. "No one has greater love than this, to lay down one's life for one's friends" (John 15:13). This is exactly what he had failed to do. Anthony Giambrone OP, of the École Biblique, translates his three replies in this way:

> "Yes, Lord, I love you more than they do and more than I love the others. You are more; you are my friend."
>
> Then, "*Phileō!* I said it and I mean it. You are my friend."
>
> Finally, "You know . . . all things, you experience . . . that I love with the full love of friendship."[2]

Note the gentle irony. Peter says, "You know me." On that sad night, he had denied he knew Jesus, but Jesus knows him better than he knows himself. According to the early legend, he would fail again during the Neronian persecution. Fleeing Rome, he met Christ going to the

2. *The Bible and the Priesthood: Priestly Participation in the One Sacrifice for Sins* (Baker Academic, 2022), 185–86.

city. He asks his Lord, "Where are you going? *Quo vadis*?" "To die again." Finally Peter shows that greatest of all loves, which he had twice professed and denied. Finally, at the end of his life, he is faithful to his vow of love. This gives courage to us all when we fail. It can take a whole lifetime to learn to live one's vows! It is not too late.

Now here is a lesson of the utmost importance for this synod. Jesus trusted Peter and entrusted the flock to him, although so far, he had been untrustworthy. The Church is founded on the rock of God's unmerited trust in Simon Peter. Will we dare to trust each other, despite some betrayals? This synod depends on it.

Just one example: It is no secret that *Fiducia Supplicans* provoked distress and anger among many bishops around the world. Some members of this synod did feel betrayed. But the Church will only become a trustworthy community if we take the risk, like the Lord, of trusting each other, even though we have been hurt. The Lord entrusts himself into our hands again and again, at every Eucharist, even though we betray him again and again. The sexual abuse crisis has taught us painfully that this cannot be an irresponsible trust that puts others, especially minors, at risk but a trust that embraces our *own* risk of getting hurt.

There is a global crisis of trust. Politicians of all parties say that the politicians of the *other* parties are not to be trusted, and so, of course, no one trusts politicians anymore. All over the world, the young are losing confidence in democracy. Fake news and the manipulation of the media mean that we cannot trust that the truth is being told. We demand more and more accountability, more tests and reports, but they can never allay our suspicion that someone is getting away with something. A crisis of trust encourages people to behave in an untrustworthy way, since everyone else is surely doing so. Clement of Alexandria wrote in the third century that we must "take the beautiful risk of passing over into God's camp."[3] That is the camp of those who trust in the Lord and each other, even when it seems foolish. We cannot say, "I am not going to risk being hurt again."

A farmer rushed up to Saint Francis of Assisi and asked him if he was Francis. The farmer then said, "I tell you, do not be other than you appear to be, for many people put their trust in you."[4] These words scare me. If only they knew! Millions no longer trust us, and with good reason. We must build trust again, beginning with each other in this assembly. Trust is the most beautiful gift we can give.

When I was elected master of the Dominicans, I asked my predecessor, a marvelous Irishman, for his

3. *Protrepticus* X, 93. Quoted in Giambrone, *The Bible and the Priesthood*, 128.

4. *Fonti Francescane* (Editrici Francescane, 2011) (my translation).

advice. He said, "First of all, when you travel in remote places, always have some lavatory paper in your back pocket."—Very wise!—"Secondly, trust the brethren. The Order has voted to trust you. You must trust the brethren. Provincials will sometimes make decisions that puzzle you and with which you disagree. Except in exceptional circumstances, trust them." Saint Dominic trusted the novices and sent them out to preach, even though the Cistercians were sure they would all run away. Trust binds Peter's net together.

One of our provincials was a fine brother, but he struggled with alcoholism. To my surprise, he was re-elected. I was proud that the provincial chapter took the risk, and I confirmed the election with joy. Though I am reminded of an American Dominican who had a problem with drink, and so he went to see his doctor. The doctor said, "Father, the very best thing that you could do would be to give up drink altogether." The brother replied, "Doctor, I am not worthy of the very best. What is the second best?"

Ultimately everything is founded on trust in God who entrusts himself to us. We trust that with the grace of God, this synod will bear fruit, even though we cannot anticipate what this will be and it may not be what we want.

A poem by Teilhard de Chardin:

> Above all, trust in the slow work of God.
> We are quite naturally impatient in everything to reach the end without delay.
> We should like to skip the intermediate stages.
> We are impatient of being on the way to something unknown, something new.
> And yet it is the law of all progress
> that it is made by passing through some stages of instability—
> and that it may take a very long time.[5]

Another Jesuit (I am in a generous mood!), Gregory Boyle again: "Ours is a God who waits. Who are we not to? It takes what it takes for the great turnabout. Wait for it."[6]

Jesus commissions Peter to pasture his sheep. "*My* sheep," Jesus says, not "your sheep." Peter is to be the good shepherd who leads the sheep out of the narrow confines of the sheepfold to feed in the broad pastures of the world, where wolves lie in wait. He knows his flock by name, and they will trust his voice. All who are baptized into the kingship of Christ are called to be pastors: pastors of the little flocks of our families, of the pupils of our

5. "Patient Trust," in Michael Harter SJ, ed., *Hearts on Fire: Praying with the Jesuits* (Loyola Press, 2009), 102. Used with permission.

6. *Tattoos on the Heart*, 113.

schools, of our next-door neighbors. Parents, teachers, lay leaders are all called to be pastors who know their sheep by name and gain their trust. We all have the extraordinary responsibility of caring for the Lord's sheep.

But Jesus gives Peter a specific role in the community as his good shepherd. Jesus' words to him are written above the altar in Saint Peter's Basilica, where we celebrated Mass last evening. This is a role particularly of our ordained pastors, to lead the sheep out of a narrow, introverted, ecclesiastical sheepfold into the wide-open spaces of the world. From the sacristy to the public square. Yet often it is the clergy who are most suspicious of the synodal path and resistant to it. What authority has Peter and his successors to do this?

Sara Paris of Edinburgh University wrote, "The authority of Peter is the authority of a repentant sinner."[7] He can lead the flock into the pasture of God's grace because he so evidently needs it himself. Pope Francis said in an interview in 2015, "I am a sinner. . . . I am sure of this. I am a sinner whom the Lord looked upon with mercy. I am, as I said to detainees in Bolivia, a forgiven man [see Luke 5:8]."[8] This is the joyful authority of the shepherds.

7. Personal communication.

8. "Intervista del Santo Padre Francesco al settimanale 'Credere,'" December 2, 2015, https://press.vatican.va/content/salastampa/it/bollettino/pubblico/2015/12/02/0952/02135.html (my translation).

We are forgiven people. We can let drop the heavy mask of superiority, the burden of pretending to be frightfully holy. The priest gathers us all into unity at the beginning of the Eucharist as we call to mind "*our* sins," not "your sins"! This is the foundation of our unity: gracious forgiveness. When someone asks to be clothed in most religious orders, there is a question: "What do you seek?" To which the reply is: "God's mercy and yours." It is therefore so appropriate, as Madre Maria Ignazia said this morning, that we celebrate a service of penitence this evening.

The joy of the repentant sinner is to step into the dawning light of God's tender judgment and discover oneself utterly loved. Cardinal Basil Hume wrote, "Judgment is whispering into the ear of a merciful and compassionate God the story of my life which I have never been able to tell." Here, the cardinal said, he was quoting an unnamed priest. Cardinal Hume went on, "Many of us have a story, or part of one at any rate, about which we have never been able to speak to anyone. Fear of being misunderstood, inability to understand ourselves, ignorance of the darker side of our hidden lives, or just shame, make it very difficult for many people. . . . What a relief it will be to be able to whisper freely and fully into that merciful and compassionate ear. After all that is what He has always wanted."[9]

9. *To Be a Pilgrim: A Spiritual Notebook* (SPCK, 1984), 228.

On the beach Peter was not yet ready explicitly to tell the story of his own need for forgiveness. That day will come. The first account we have of Peter's denial of Jesus is in Mark's gospel, which is often called Peter's memoirs. Saint Mark knew of Peter's failure because Peter shared it with him. During the Neronian persecution, the Church largely collapsed, and Christians betrayed each other. It seems it was then that Peter owned up to his own failure: "You betrayed the Lord. So did I!" The *Instrumentum Laboris* says that often we have demanded that the people of God be accountable to the hierarchy, but the hierarchy must be accountable to the people of God, too (see IL 75, 76). In the darkest time, Peter gave an account of himself to his people. This turned his shame into joy. This is the shepherd's ministry of unity, to gather us forgiven sinners together so that we "dare to say 'Our Father.'" Clerical elitism is thus not just a lack of humility but a negation of priestly identity. It would be like being a gardener who thought his job was to pull up the flowers or a clown who does not want people even to smile.

Peter finally, at the end, achieves that greatest act of love. "No one has greater love than this, to lay down one's life for one's friends" (John 15:13). The priest is the minister of the divine friendship. The *Instrumentum Laboris* warns us that priests often speak of "a certain fatigue, linked above all to a sense of isolation, loneliness, being cut off from healthy and sustainable relationships, and of being overwhelmed by the demand to provide answers to every need" (IL 35). The synod looks like one more thing to be done by people who are already busy beyond bearing.

The temptation of the priest is to be a loner, doing everything himself. But this contradicts his vocation, the call to friendship: a friend of God, friendship with the laity, friendship with those on the edge, friendship with other priests in the presbyterium. Saint Antony the Great became in the desert the friend of all, because he achieved transparency. Peter Brown wrote, "He came to radiate such magnetic charm and openness to all, that any stranger who came upon him, surrounded by crowds of disciples, visiting monks, and lay pilgrims, knew which one was the great Antony. He was instantly recognizable as someone whose heart had achieved total transparency to others."[10]

This is why a failure of transparency and accountability corrupts the very heart of the priestly identity. The transparency of Peter the sinner is the foundation of his authority. There can be no cover-up. We are not expected to openly confess all of our sins—thanks be to God—but at least not to be hypocrites. The people of God are speedy to forgive all else except hypocrisy.

10. Quoted in Michael Heher, *The Lost Art of Walking on Water: Reimagining the Priesthood* (Paulist, 2004), 70.

"No one has greater love than this, to lay down one's life for one's friends." Many priests feel that they do indeed lay down their lives, giving their all, burnt out and exhausted. When an English priest, Sean Connolly, was young, he wrote, "Sometimes I feel like a giant sponge, soaking up their difficulties and trials. The problem is that there is often nowhere to squeeze myself out and so it all just builds up and builds up." He has friends who left the priesthood because they wanted to have their lives back. Teachers at the end of the week shout out to him, "Have a nice weekend." A nice weekend, for goodness' sake! He says, "Driving home on a Friday afternoon sometimes, the thought does cross my mind: wouldn't it be nice to have my own life again."[11] Now Father Sean has found again fully the joy of his priesthood.

Jesus did *not* say, "I have come that you may survive and survive abundantly." Remember, *Gloria Dei homo vivens*—the glory of God is a human being fully alive. Laying down your life does not mean laying down your daily diary. It is not doing everything by oneself.

Cardinal Ratzinger quoted Jesus' words to Peter at the funeral of John Paul II: "Someone else will fasten a belt around you" (John 21:18). The cardinal continued, "And in this very communion with the suffering Lord, tirelessly and with renewed intensity, [John Paul II] pro-

11. *Simple Priesthood* (St Paul's, 2001), 27, 42.

claimed the Gospel, the mystery of that love which goes to the end (cf. *Jn* 13:1)."[12] Laying down your life is an act of love, not endless work. Friendship is learning to be with people and delight in their company. It is shared leisure and laughter, as when Jesus feasted with the prostitutes and tax collectors.

So Peter has the authority of the repentant sinner. But this is not the only authority in this passage. Jesus tells Peter, "Follow me." Peter looks at the disciple whom Jesus loved and who is *already* following the Lord. "What about him?" Peter asks. "What is it to you?'" Jesus replies. The Beloved Disciple has his own authority. He saw the empty tomb and he believed. We have been studying his witness and "we know that his testimony is true" (John 21:24). On the cross Jesus consigns his mother to John's care. Yesterday James Martin SJ suggested to me that the Beloved Disciple might be Lazarus. I found this an exciting idea which I must explore.

Each defers to the authority of the other. Peter recognizes the authority of the Beloved Disciple on the night before Jesus dies, when he asks him to ask Jesus who will betray him. It is probably the Beloved Disciple who had the authority to gain Peter entrance to the high priest's

12. "Funeral Mass of the Roman Pontiff John Paul II: Homily of His Eminence Card. Joseph Ratzinger," April 8, 2005, https://www.vatican.va/gpII/documents/homily-card-ratzinger_20050408_en.html.

house. But the Beloved Disciple defers to Peter, too. He runs to the tomb and arrives there first, but he defers to Peter's seniority and lets him enter first.

The role of shepherds is to be self-effacing and to honor the authority of everyone in their care. Everyone has something to offer. Vincent Donovan was a missionary priest who worked with the Masai in East Africa. For a long time, he puzzled over his priestly role. He discovered that

> he would not be the one in the community who knew the most theology, the theologian. He would not be the preacher or the evangelist of the community. He would not be the prophet. He would not be the most important member in the community, in the sense of being the one who was to make the most important contribution, of which the community might someday be capable. But he would be the focal point of the whole community, the one who would enable the community to act, whether in worship or in service. . . . He would be the sign of their union with the outside, the universal church. He would be their priest.[13]

13. *Christianity Rediscovered: An Epistle from the Masai* (Fides, 1978), 144–45.

The successors of the Beloved Disciple are all those whose eyes are opened to spot the stranger on the beach and declare, "It is the Lord." This is their authority. Mother Teresa saw the Lord dying on the streets of Kolkata. Mary Magdalene has her authority, too, as the one to whom the Risen Lord first spoke, the apostle to the apostles. Her tender love opens her to encounter his presence. Thomas has authority because of his passion for the truth. Each defers to the other. Rivalry is the enemy of good authority in the Church. A holy hermit in the desert repelled all the attacks of a pack of demons. But Satan came and whispered in his ear, "Your brother has been made Bishop of Alexandria." The holy hermit exploded in fury. "That's how it is done," said Satan!

So in this synod, may we discern each other's authority and defer to it. What new ministries are needed for the Church to recognize people's authority and commission them to exercise it? The gospel sheds light on so many who acted with authority then. May we do so today. For *today* is the only day we have. *Carpe diem!*

Listening in Silence Together

We begin today in the synod to think about the processes through which Church changes, the pathways we need. The following strange text offers some insight into how this happens:

> Jesus left that place and went away to the district of Tyre and Sidon. Just then a Canaanite woman from that region came out and started shouting, "Have mercy on me, Lord, Son of David; my daughter is tormented by a demon." But he did not answer her at all. And his disciples came and urged him, saying, "Send her away, for she keeps shouting after us." He answered, "I was sent only to the lost sheep of the house of Israel." But she came and knelt before him, saying, "Lord, help me." He answered, "It is not fair to take the children's food

> and throw it to the dogs." She said, "Yes, Lord, yet even the dogs eat the crumbs that fall from their masters' table." Then Jesus answered her, "Woman, great is your faith! Let it be done for you as you wish." And her daughter was healed instantly. (Matt 15:21-28)

At first sight it looks as if Jesus is being rude, calling her a dog. And that he only makes an exception for the Canaanite woman's daughter because of her personal faith. "I have come only to the lost sheep of Israel and, all right, *you*."

But this incident belongs to the evolution of Jesus' mission. It comes between the feeding of the five thousand, which symbolizes the mission to the Jews, and the feeding of the four thousand, which points to the mission to the Gentiles. Jesus had told the woman there was only enough bread for the children of the household, but a few verses later there will be more than enough bread for everyone, seven baskets full of leftovers.

The center of this encounter is silence. She makes her request and, the gospel says, "He did not answer her at all." The disciples say, "Send her away." They have an immediate solution to her question. Get rid of her. Silence her. But it is Jesus who is silent.

Jesus' silences are never empty. He is silent when they bring to him the woman caught in adultery. He is silent during the trial before his death. His silence faced with the woman is not a rebuff. He is listening to his Father and to her. It is the silence in which something new is germinating. As the Irish poet Yeats wrote, "Like a long-legged fly upon the stream / His mind moves upon silence."[1]

Remember Madre Maria Ignazia's beautiful meditation on "To you, silence is praise" (the beginning of Psalm 64). "At the root of every prayer, of every 'work for God,' vibrates the silent Breath of God. It is a matter of perceiving it."[2]

In the Old Testament, silence is a sign of wisdom, the refusal to be caught up in unthinking responses. Rowan Williams talks of "the silence that emerges because of a steady refusal of the uncritical agenda of the ego."[3] This is the pregnant silence when one refuses to impose one's own will, one's language, but waits for words that will give space to the other person. Just as Jesus writes silently in

1. William Butler Yeats, "Long-Legged Fly," https://allpoetry.com/Long-Legged-Fly.

2. Mother Maria Ignazia Angelini, "Synod Retreat Meditation: 'To You, Silence Is Praise'—Full Text," October 1, 2024, https://www.vaticannews.va/en/vatican-city/news/2024-10/synod-retreat-meditation-mother-angelini-to-you-silence-praise.html.

3. *The Edge of Words: God and the Habits of Language* (Bloomsbury Continuum, 2014), 234.

the sand before he speaks to those who wish to stone the woman caught in adultery.

Our synodal assemblies have been filled with silence, as we listen to the Lord and each other. Many people demand a quick decision on, for example, the ordination of women to the diaconate or the opening of the priesthood to married men. But the silence on such issues is not that of denial but of listening for the right way forward. In a society of instant communication, demanding immediate responses, we need the space quietly to play with new ways of thinking, to be tentative, to imagine. The archbishop of Salzburg reported that when he asked young people what they wanted of the Church, they replied that "church should be a place where you can talk, where what you say doesn't immediately make the rounds like it usually does on the internet."[4]

People demand a yes or no. Can the Canaanite woman's daughter be healed? Yes or no. Can women become deacons? Yes or no. But that would be to remain in the same binary logic, the same discourse. In the gospels, the way forward is usually through the breakthrough into a new language, a new imagination in which ancient categories are transcended.

4. Archbishop Franz Lackner, from the report on the European presynodal workshop in Linz, 2024.

In this story, the breakthrough takes the form of a strange dialogue: "It is not fair to take the children's food and throw it to the dogs." "Yes, Lord, yet even the dogs eat the crumbs that fall from their masters' table." This looks offensive. How could Jesus refer to this woman and her daughter as dogs? But it is not. Matthew has taken this incident from Mark, in which the woman is Syrophoenician. At the site of the ancient Syrophoenician city of Ashkelon, in Israel, a cemetery for seven hundred dogs was discovered. They were small dogs that had died of natural causes from the fifth to third centuries BC.[5] It seems the dogs of the ancient Syrophoenician people who buried them there were their best friends, treasured members of their household. Just like the dogs of the English are today!

So in this gospel account, a new way of being a household is imagined, in which the woman and her daughter have a place. For the Jews, dogs were unclean animals who had no place in the household. They are outside the door, like those who licked the wounds of Lazarus. Jesus reaches out to the woman with her own idea of what a household should be like, in which dogs have their place, as in most English households!

5. See Lawrence E. Stager, "Why Were Hundreds of Dogs Buried at Ashkelon?," *Biblical Archaeology Review* 17 (1991): 27–42.

Many people are watching this synod, expecting a yes or no on various issues! But the challenge is to be more creative. We need to imagine new ways of being together, new images of the household in which we can dwell together in mutual respect. What new ministries might we imagine? We shall only do so if we learn how to be silent, listening to the Lord and each other, opening ourselves to new ways of talking. The disciples want to get rid of awkward questions. "Silence this woman and her awkward questions!" We have to welcome awkward questions, especially those to which we have no immediate answer. Many are coming from women!

The Freedom of Those Who Trust

We are about to embark on our last task as a synod: to consider the final document, amend it, and vote on it. Today we prepare ourselves to exercise this weighty responsibility. How are we to do so?

With freedom! Saint Paul wrote to the Galatians, "For freedom Christ has set us free" (5:1). Our mission is to preach and embody this freedom. Freedom is the double helix of the Christian DNA. First of all, it is the freedom to say what we believe and to listen without fear to what others say, in mutual respect. This is the freedom of the children of God to speak boldly, with *parrésia* (see, e.g., Acts 4:29), as the disciples boldly declared the good news of the resurrection in Jerusalem. Because of this freedom, each of us can say, "I." We do not have the right to keep silent.

This freedom is rooted in a deeper freedom, the interior freedom of our hearts as we discover the decisions that are taken. We may be disappointed with the decisions of the synod. Some of us will consider these to be ill-advised or even wrong. But we have the freedom of those who believe that, as Saint Paul wrote to the Romans, "All things work together for good for those who love God" (Rom 8:28). And, we hope, even for those who do not! We can be at peace because "nothing can separate us from the love of God," not even incompetence, not even mistakes. Because of this freedom, we can dare to belong to the Church and say, "We."

The heart of our decision-making is this double helix of graced freedom. For God's freedom operates in the very depths of our own free thinking and deciding. Saint Thomas Aquinas taught that grace perfects nature. It does not destroy it. When Saint Thomas asked himself how the wise men managed to get to Bethlehem so quickly, he concluded that it was due to the grace of God and the speed of the dromedaries![1]

Let us consider briefly each dimension of this graced freedom. A priest once began his homily at the Sunday evening Mass saying, "Before this morning's Mass, I had no time to prepare, and so I had to rely on the Holy Spirit. Now I have had time to think for myself, and so I hope to do better!" He was not a Dominican or even a

1. "Partim quidem adducti divina virtute, partim autem dromedariorum velocitate" (*ST* III, q. 31, art. 6, ad. 3).

Jesuit! Belief in the Holy Spirit does not excuse us from using our minds as we search for the truth. Thomas asserted that it would be an insult to the Holy Spirit not to think about decisions and, for example, draw lots. Vivian Boland OP said, "We are children of God so that in our thinking, desiring, fearing, and preferring, the Holy Spirit, too, is at work."[2]

In the play *A Man for All Seasons*, Saint Thomas More implores his daughter Meg to honor our God-given ability to think: "God made the angels to show him splendour—as he made animals for innocence and plants for their simplicity. But Man He made to serve Him wittily [intelligently], in the tangle of his mind!"[3]

Yves Congar was silenced by Rome. He was even exiled to England, a terrible fate for a Frenchman! Strangely, he never appreciated our cuisine. In the depths of this crisis, he wrote in his diary that the only response to this persecution was "to speak the truth. Prudently, without provocative and useless scandal. But to remain—and to become more and more—an authentic and pure witness of that which is *true*."[4]

2. Unpublished homily for the Fourth Sunday of Easter, Year A.

3. Robert Bolt, *A Man for All Seasons: A Play of Sir Thomas More* (Bloomsbury, 1996; orig. 1960), 74.

4. *Journal of a Theologian 1946–1956*, trans. Denis Minns OP (ATF Theology, 2015), 340.

We need not be afraid of disagreement, for the Holy Spirit is at work in it. One day a man came to his rabbi to complain about his wife. At the end of the conversation, the rabbi said to him, "My friend, you are absolutely right, you are justified!" That afternoon the wife of the man came to the rabbi and complained about her husband at great length. At the end of the conversation, the rabbi said to the woman, "My friend, you are absolutely right, you are justified!" When the woman was gone, the rabbi's wife said to him, "But you're absolutely mistaken. You cannot say that both of them are right, that both of them justified." And the rabbi said to his wife, "You are right!"

So this is our freedom, to think, speak, and listen without fear. But this is nothing unless we also have the freedom of those who trust that "all things work together for good for those who love God." So we may be at peace with whatever is the result. As the fourteenth-century English mystic Julian of Norwich famously said, "All shall be well; all manner of things shall be well." God's providence is gently, silently at work, even when things seem to go wrong.

God's providence is woven into the story of our salvation from the beginning. The fall of Adam and Eve becomes, through God's grace, the *felix culpa* that leads to the incarnation. The hideous death of Our Lord on the cross leads to Christ's triumph over death.

So even if you are disappointed by the result of the synod, God's providence is at work in this assembly, bringing us to the Kingdom in ways that God alone knows. His will for our good cannot be frustrated. During the retreat, I quoted Cardinal Consalvi's reply to the alarmed monsignor who said that Napoleon wished to destroy the Church: "Not even we have succeeded in doing that." When Abraham thought he was required to kill his beloved only son, the Lord provided the ram stuck in the bushes. "On the mount of the LORD it shall be provided" (Gen 22:14).

Often we can have no idea how God's providence is at work in our lives. We do what we believe to be right, and the rest is in the hands of the Lord. This is just one synod. There will be others. We do not have to do everything, just try to take the next step. Saint Teresa of Avila wrote at the end of her long and difficult life, "It is we who have begun the work; it is up to those who follow to keep on beginning."[5] How we do not know. That is not our business.

Like Congar, Henri de Lubac SJ endured persecution prior to the council. But in the midst of that suffering, between 1945 and 1950, he wrote the beautiful and serene *Méditation sur l'Eglise*, a hymn of love to the same Church that was persecuting him. He wrote, "Far from

5. Quoted in Prakash Anthony Lohale OP and Kevin Toomey OP, eds., *Dialogue as Mission: Remembering Chrys McVey*, 2nd ed. (New Priory Press, 2014), 55.

losing patience, [the person who is persecuted] will try to keep the peace and, for his own part, make a big effort to do that hard thing—retain a *mind bigger than its own ideas.* He will cultivate 'that sort of freedom through which we transcend what involves us most remorselessly.' . . . He will [avoid] the terrible self-sufficiency which might lead him to see himself as the incarnate norm of orthodoxy, for he will put 'the indissoluble bond of Catholic peace' above all things."[6] I hope that he will be canonized soon!

If we have only the freedom to argue for our positions, we shall be tempted by the arrogance of those who, in the words of de Lubac, see themselves as "the incarnate norm of orthodoxy." We shall end up beating the drums of ideology, whether of the left or the right.

If we have only the freedom of those who trust in God's providence but dare not wade into the debate with our own convictions, we shall be irresponsible and never grow up. God's freedom works in the core of our freedom, welling up within us. The more that it is truly of God, the more it is truly our own. As the free children of God, we can each say, "I" and together say, "We."

6. *The Splendor of the Church*, trans. Michael Mason (Ignatius Press, 1986), 253–54 (emphasis mine). The first internal quotation is of Jacques Maritain; the second is of Saint Cyprian.

The Synod: What Is Happening?

It is a great joy for me to be back here in Columbus with the Dominican Sisters of Peace.[1] It is hard to imagine that soon you will be celebrating your sixteenth birthday! In fact, if one added together the ages of all the congregations that have come together—eight, I think—you are probably as old as Abraham and Sarah were when they had their promised child Isaac. So you are both old and young, and who knows to what child of promise you will give birth!

I was asked to talk about the Synod on Synodality. I expect that you have had innumerable talks on the synod, and so it is hard to know what to share. Let's begin with

1. This chapter and the following one are the texts of two addresses delivered by Cardinal Radcliffe as the featured speaker at the Founded Ministries Meeting of the Dominican Sisters of Peace, of Columbus, Ohio, on January 21, 2025.—Ed.

the reaction of a lot of my friends who are women and who feel disappointed. Nothing much seems to have happened. A three-year process of listening, the greatest listening exercise in the history of humanity, seems to have given birth to a mouse. A Dominican sister whom I admire enormously wrote to me: "The synod's message on women was disappointing—to put it mildly. I remain astounded by the persistence of the 'women should be raised up in leadership with their unique gifts' line as a dodge of the ordination issue. . . . So many of my women friends have left the church because that apparently calcified position just keeps getting reinforced." Ineffective words, empty wishes, a waste of time.

Let me be clear. I am all in favor of the ordination of women to the diaconate. I can see no convincing theological argument against it. In Oxford forty years ago, we regularly had Dominican sisters on the rota to preach at Mass. I long for that to happen again. But I do understand Pope Francis's belief that first of all a profound transformation of the Church needs to happen if this is to be lifegiving and not just more of the same.

The Church needs a profound conversion. It needs to be freed from what Pope Francis calls the cancer, the poison, of clericalism. Just before I came here, a married permanent deacon from Asia came to see me. In his country, the cardinal has ruled that there are to be no married deacons and no female altar servers. Most dioceses in the world do not accept permanent deacons. Almost half of all permanent deacons are in the United States. In most of the Church, the ordination of women to the diaconate would have no effect, since deacons are not accepted, except as a step on the way to priesthood.

Outside my bedroom, a neighboring Oxford college is demolishing some ugly old flats. For the last few months, siestas have been impossible, which leaves me very bad tempered, since siestas are sacred. In Italy, they say that a good religious gets up at 5:30, twice a day! But after all this endless noise, now there is nothing left. No new beautiful buildings. All this must happen before the new beautiful buildings can rise from the ground.

That is a little bit like where we are. The rebirth of the Church requires a vast conversion of mind and heart. We are at the beginning of a new epoch, and the Church needs to be renewed humanly and spiritually, if it is to flourish. *Being* alive means mutuality. The motto of the synod was "Where two or three are gathered in my name, I am there among them" (Matt 18:20).

Contrary to a deeply individualistic Western culture, which thinks of the human being as a solitary being, our faith is that I can only be myself with and for others. To be human is to be relational. Not Descartes's "*Cogito, ergo sum*"—"I think, therefore I am"—but as they say in Africa, "I am because we are." Throughout its history, the Church has been renewed by learning again and again to listen to God and each other. The eternal battle is against human narcissism and egocentrism. As Bette Midler famously said in *Beaches*, "But enough about me. Let's talk about you. What do *you* think of me?" This is especially difficult for us Westerners to understand. Our understanding of dialogue has been described as "negotiated self-interest." Me, me, me. From the iPhone to the iPad.

So this synod was first of all about what it means to be alive. I had been to three previous synods, in which we sat in semicircles facing the pope. I called it an ecclesiology of hats: a white hat in the middle, a couple of circles of red hats, then the purple ones, and then the ranks of the unhatted. People read aloud pre-prepared talks. There was little discussion. One bishop said that it was as exciting as an intercontinental flight without the movies.

Now it was utterly different. At the tables, groups of ten or eleven people—cardinals, lay men and women, religious—listened to each other in silence. Each person spoke for the same amount of time. After every few interventions, we paused in silence, to listen to the Lord and meditate on what each person had said. I have never been to a meeting that was so filled with silence. Some bishops admitted that they had never really listened before. Not only bishops.

In Deuteronomy, God says to his people, "I have set before you life and death. . . . Choose life" (30:19). Saint Irenaeus in the second century famously wrote, "*Gloria Dei homo vivens*"—"The glory of God is a human being fully alive." The Church will be renewed when people look at Christians and think, "Wow, these people are mysteriously alive." As I have often said, my own religious vocation was awakened by a Benedictine great uncle who was a chaplain in the First World War. He was a brave man who went every night into no-man's-land to look for the wounded. He lost an eye and most of the fingers on one hand. But he was alive with a joy that could only come from God. When I told him that I wanted to become a Dominican, he said, "They are terribly intelligent. I don't expect they will accept you." I squeezed in!

We come alive in mutuality. The baby receives the gift of self from its parents' faces and words. We all come alive as we encounter God in each other. So of course, the Word became flesh in a human being who delighted in conversation. I quote the final document of the synod: "Jesus never sent anyone away without stopping to listen and to speak to them, whether men or women, Jews or pagans, doctors of the law or publicans, righteous men and women or sinners, beggars, the blind, lepers or the sick. By meeting people wherever their history and personal freedom had led them, He revealed to them the face of the Father."[2] Ours is a religion of faces, which are made to smile.

2. Pope Francis and XVI Ordinary General Assembly of the Synod of Bishops, *For a Synodal Church: Communion, Participation, Mission: Final Document*, October 26, 2024, no. 51, https://www.synod.va/content/dam

In the synod, barriers began to crumble. People opened themselves to others. Friendships were born. James Martin SJ found that people became less nervous about him and his ministry to LGBT people. People stopped calling each other by exotic ecclesiastical titles like Eminence. Though I am beginning to think that is rather a fine title! Though one cardinal reminded me that in French, *eminence* means only a small hill.

People used their baptismal names, for there is no greater dignity than to be baptized. At the first assembly, relationships between many African bishops and Western members were tense. This time, relationships thawed, spring began.

Now I expect you may be getting impatient. All this listening and friendship business is lovely, but will it really change the Church? Will it make any difference to the place of the laity and especially women in the Church? I shall look at some of these issues more closely in the second lecture, especially how all this relates to issues of gender, priests and the laity, and the encounter of other cultures. But just a few preliminary remarks.

Pope Francis removed some contentious topics from the discussion and assigned them to ten working groups: ministries in the Church, the role of the women, the

---

/synod/news/2024-10-26_final-document/ENG---Documento-finale.pdf.

selection and ministry of bishops, relationships with Eastern churches, and so on. The cynics think that this is a way of making sure that nothing changes. Park a topic with a commission, and it will die. I did this when I was master of the Dominicans. The cardinal in charge of liturgy was unhappy with a new breviary just published by the Province of Saint Albert the Great and wanted it suppressed. I appointed a commission to study the issue. I am not sure that it ever met. When I arrived in Rome, I had no idea how to engage with the Vatican. I went to ask the superior general of the Jesuits, Peter Hans Kolvenbach. He said that it was like playing tennis. Keep the ball in the air!

But the cynics are wrong. These two synodal assemblies are just part of a vast, complex process by which the Church is renewed humanly and so divinely. This requires at least three things: transparency, accountability, and the reception of teaching by the people of God. Clericalism, which Pope Francis detests, rejects all three.

Transparency: After the Fall, Adam and Eve fled from the sight of God and hid. They were ashamed to be naked in each other's sight. Redemption means that we dare to show ourselves as we are. Of course, we do not have to confess all our sins to the community, thanks be to God. But we need not hide. At baptism in the early Church, one was naked, a sort of return to the unashamed nakedness before the Fall.

The Holy See is founded on two people who dared to be seen as they are. In the gospels, Peter is presented as someone who denied his Lord in his hour of need and Paul as a murderer of early Christians. Only God could have such a crazy idea to found a community on two such pillars. It means that there is a place for us all. Clericalism means that a priest hides behind his role. We have seen the devastating consequences of cover-up in the Church. The face becomes a mask.

So do we dare be transparent to each other within our own religious communities? Do we help priests to be transparent and share their doubts, fears, hopes, and failures? Synodality means inviting each other to step out into the light. I love Emily Dickinson's poem "I'm Nobody! Who are you?" All new priests should learn it by heart. Well, anyone in leadership.

> I'm Nobody! Who are you?
> Are you – Nobody – too?
> Then there's a pair of us!
> Don't tell! they'd advertise – you know!
>
> How dreary – to be – Somebody!
> How public – like a Frog –
> To tell one's name – the livelong June –
> To an admiring Bog![3]

3. "I'm Nobody! Who are you?," in *The Poems of Emily Dickinson: Reading Edition* (The Belknap Press of Harvard University Press, 1998).

Mutuality also means mutual accountability. The Church has long insisted that the people of God be accountable to the hierarchy. The new insistence of the synod is that the hierarchy, the Roman Curia, everyone, be accountable to the people of God. Already at the synod, we began to see this happening. There was a lot of anger over Study Group 5, which was supposed to look at the ordination of women to the diaconate. When members of the synod went to hear a report, they were met by two junior officials who were there just to take notes. No interaction. The members of the synod were furious. Why was the prefect of the dicastery not there? And so a meeting with him was speedily arranged with eighty people, and a good discussion was had. He had to apologize and render account. He had to listen to people's anger. And what was really extraordinary: the Vatican publicly released a recording of the encounter. This would have been unimaginable a few years ago. This is a new way of being Church.

Then there is reception. The people of God must be consulted, and their views must be taken into account. There are supposed to be diocesan and parochial councils of all sorts. Often they do not meet. The synod insisted that they be mandatory and effective. The hierarchy must listen. Cardinal McElroy said, "If the people in the community, in proper discernment, come to a conclusion, you cannot lightly or without accountability take another pathway without telling them this and explaining and having a further dialogue."[4] The people of God have a connatural understanding of the faith.

When Cardinal Tobin went to a new diocese, he was asked what *his* plan for the diocese was. He replied that he did not have one. Shock, horror, indignation. Then he explained: We, the whole diocese, would elaborate a plan. We Westerners are captured by business models that see everything in terms of executive power rather than organic flourishing. There was a bishop of Kerry in Ireland who said after the council, "In this diocese, we are all equal—from me downwards"!

So you can see why, for Pope Francis, clericalism is the great obstacle to the renewal of the Church. It withdraws us priests from the mutuality that is our sharing in the life of God. Pope Francis embodies this mutuality in his very being. Many participants were nervous about any talk of welcoming LGBT people. Rather than making a statement, the pope welcomed the leaders of the New Ways Ministry, who have reached out to gay people for decades. He welcomed and listened to a group of transgender people. When I was named a cardinal, I was deeply apprehensive, because I did not wish in any

4. Gerald O'Connell, "Interview: Why Cardinal McElroy Is 'Very Happy' with the Results of the Synod," *America*, November 1, 2024, https://www.americamagazine.org/faith/2024/11/01/cardinal-mcelroy-synod-synodality-249170.

way to lose my rooting in the brotherhood of the Order. Before I had time to ask, he proposed that as a cardinal, I should just go on wearing the habit as a brother; he understood before I said a word.

Synodality cannot happen unless the clergy willingly embrace it with joy. For this we need a non-clericalist but highly affirmative vision of the ordained priesthood. This is not the place to elaborate it, and I am not the person to do so. But surely at its heart is an understanding of the priest's call to friendship. Here the Dominican tradition has so much to offer. For Aquinas, our love of God was entering into the eternal friendship of the Trinity. An English provincial a hundred years ago, Bede Jarrett, said it was the most beautiful thing on earth. Other orders told their young members to be nervous about particular friends. We were told to beware of particular enmities!

So the synod is a call for conversion. Near the beginning, we had a deeply moving penitential service, in which cardinal after cardinal came forward and confessed the sins of the Church. "*Chiedo perdono, provando vergona*"—"I ask for pardon, experiencing shame." Many of us wept both for shame at the Church's sins, our sins, and for joy at this moment of grace.

How can we share this moment of conversion with the Church and the world? A long, dry document was produced, voted on, and amended. Considering that all this was done in a couple of days, it was an amazing achievement. But it probably will not set people's hearts on fire.

It is hard to grasp what the synod is about because the transformation it invites is deeply countercultural. The challenge is rather like that of talking about sex with someone who is just at the beginning of puberty. When I was a young lad at my Benedictine school, an elderly monk took me aside for what was called "The Jaw," an explanation of the facts of life, the birds and the bees. For some reason, I got the idea that he was talking about Winston Churchill. When the penny dropped, I thought it all sounded too absurd and ridiculous, which is just what many people think of the synod. Sex and the synod (a new TV series?)—both concern an intimacy that one must *live* if one is to understand it. The synod was living a new intimacy.

Part of the problem was the complex relationship between the synod and the media. The media reported on the synod, but the members of the synod read the media and received from media an interpretation of what they were doing. I avidly read excellent journalists like Chris White in the *National Catholic Reporter*. The synod was an event in the digital world and not just in the synod hall. But a lot of the media see everything through the lens of conflict, of fear, of battles for power. So the synod is completely incomprehensible to these journalists. Its vision of transformative face-to-face encounter is simply too countercultural. And we members of the synod were also reading their accounts of what we were up to—and half-believing them! When you read in the media that it is all a disappointment, it is hard not to think that it is, even if you are actually having a wonderful experience of grace.

Much of the media loves stoking up conflict. Let me give you a tiny example. I wrote an article in *The Tablet* last April, arguing that we must understand the reaction of the African bishops to the proposal for blessings of gay couples. I noted that they are under pressure from evangelicals funded by American money, from the Russian Orthodox Church funded by Putin, and from Islamicists funded by Middle Eastern regimes. This was misreported as saying that their reactions were dictated by the need to get funding, which has no connection with what I wrote. Suddenly I found that the African bishops, whom I had been defending, were furious with me, and there were plans to denounce me to the synod. Thanks be to God, I managed to meet Cardinal Ambongo and explain it all, and he defended me in a press briefing half an hour later.

Trying to share the synodal call to mutuality through a media that is usually dedicated to promoting conflict and anger is like trying to make ice cream in the Sahara.

A last, brief point on mutuality. At the beginning of the first assembly, I thought that the greatest obstacle to life-giving mutuality was the polarization of the

Church between traditionalists and progressives. That is the schism within much of the West, especially in the United States. I have never used dating apps, you will be pleased to know. But I am told the first question is usually whether you vote Democrat or Republican. So we tend to think in terms of which side wins. This radical opposition between tradition and progress is utterly alien to Catholicism. It is often described as a fruit of the Enlightenment, which was not always so enlightening.

As the synod progressed, I began to think that the real challenge to mutuality was much more profound and exciting. It was intercultural. The Church is becoming ever more global, more catholic. We Westerners are becoming a minority. How can the Church become truly intercultural?

This is a truly profound vocation in a world that is being engulfed ever more deeply by war and violence. One in five members of the synod came from countries at war. How can we liberate our minds from the arrogance of those who believe that we are destined to rule the world? As members of our international Order, we have a special role to play.

Our beloved sister Margaret Ormond discovered this as she loved Dominican Sisters International into being. She described once how an encounter on a rubbish site outside San Salvador changed her life:

> When I saw the garbage site where the people lived, I was overcome by tears. I tried to hide my tears and just catch my breath so that I could carry on without much notice. But, a little girl, who was probably about 6, saw me crying. She reached up, waved a hand to call me down to where she could touch me and she wiped away my tears. She showed me compassion in a way that was transforming because after that I knew I had to move beyond my backyard. She was the one who led me to discover my international vocation.[5]

In this talk, I have stressed mutuality, relationality. This is what it means to be human, and it is, therefore, what it means to be Church. Next, we need to look at how we live that mutuality in the context of difference; differences between men and women; differences of culture in a Church that stretches across space and time; differences within the people of God, hierarchy and laity. The clue here will be reciprocity. So from mutuality to reciprocity.

5. Patrizia Morgante, "An Interview with Sr. Margaret Ormond, OP," *International Dominican Information*, no. 452 (May 2007): 123.

Reciprocity Is the Key

The heart of synodality is mutuality. "Where two or three are gathered in my name, I am there among them" (Matt 18:20). Mutuality means transparency, accountability, and acknowledgment that the people of God have received the Holy Spirit. As Saint John said, "[Y]ou have been anointed by the Holy One, and all of you have knowledge" (1 John 2:20).

This mutuality implies equality. We share in the equal love of the Trinity. But all through the discussion of the synod, we were puzzling over a constant theme, sometimes explicitly but often implicitly, perhaps only half aware of it. What does this life-giving mutuality mean when we are equal but different—as women and men, as ordained and lay, as members of different cultures? In all cases, different but equal. All three of those cases touch the question of the ordination of women to the diaconate. Women and men, lay and ordained, and for a Church in which most dioceses do not even accept the ordination of male permanent deacons.

I confess that I had never thought much about this before. I instinctively thought in terms of complementarity. It was Professor Anna Rowlands, an English theologian, who first challenged me on the inadequacy of this approach, for example, between men and women. We need a new way of speaking. I went around the synod hall, nagging everyone as to what this could be and was never satisfied with the answers I received.

Then one day I was stopped by Lucca. Lucca is an Italian fisherman who now rescues migrants from the sea. He thrust into my hands an article from *L'Osservatore Romano*, by an Italian theologian, Chiara Giaccardi. The title was "Reciprocity: This Is the Key Word."[1] She was right. Slowly I became convinced that it was reciprocity. I think that it is the very heart of synodality. It is everywhere present in the final document.

Instead of being constrained by fixed, predetermined, complementary roles, as if we were jigsaw pieces being fitted together, we flourish in reciprocity. For example, I quote the final document: "We are . . . called to experience how practicing the new commandment of recipro-

1. September 28, 2024, https://www.osservatoreromano.va/en/news/2024-10/dcm-009/reciprocity-this-is-the-key-word.html.

cal love is the place and form of encounter with God" (*For a Synodal Church*, 44).

Reciprocity means we discover who we are through and with the other person. It is a dynamic relationship. In the family, the "domestic church," parents discover what it means to be mothers and fathers through their children, and the children learn the meaning of childhood with and from their parents. My mother said she joked she could stop being a mother when all six of her children left home. But even on her deathbed, she showed what it means to be a mother as she reflected on what she might still do for her children. And twenty years later, her children are still learning from her what it means to be her children and, in their turn, parents.

Reciprocal relationships are evolving, open to surprise. Reciprocity comes from a Latin word meaning "to move backwards and forwards." It implies fluid interplay. Think of the waves of the sea in constant motion, each wave forming the other in unending aqueous dialogue. I like that phrase! Unending aqueous dialogue.

Just before the synod, Pope Francis provoked outrage during a visit to Belgium by words he spoke about his vision of the relationship of men and women. The president of the Catholic University of Louvain described the position of the Church as "incomprehensible." No scholar should ever say that something is incomprehensible, only that they do not comprehend it. Mary

McAleese, the former president of Ireland, has described Pope Francis's views on gender identity as "misogynist drivel." Which is not exactly a synodal reaction.

Commenting on the disastrous visit to Louvain, the journalist Jean-Pierre Denis commented, "The pope may not fully grasp how deeply our culture believes that each person defines their own origin, purpose, and standards. Contrary to what he preaches and hopes for, the individual has overtaken the concept of the person. . . . In a society where gender issues are increasingly central and where male dominance over women is being questioned everywhere, the incident in Louvain should serve as a wake-up call. Thinking about women the way Saint John Paul II did is no longer possible."[2]

So on the one hand, there is the language, at least implicitly, of complementarity, which seems to be too static. On the other is that of identity as constructed, chosen. The American dream is that you can be whoever or whatever you wish, a consumer choice. As the star of the recent film *The Brutalist* has said, "I am who I am. Not who you want."[3] This is claimed as a right, like the right to own your body.

2. Jean-Pierre Denis, "Pope Francis and the Louvain Deadlock," *La-Croix International*, October 3, 2024, https://international.la-croix.com/opinions/pope-francis-and-the-louvain-deadlock.

3. Jake Coyle, " 'The Brutalist,' 'Emilia Perez' Triumph at Golden Globes," Associated Press, January 6, 2025, https://www.ap.org/news

Neither seems correct. For Christians, identity is neither chosen nor simply fixed. It is discovered as one responds to the summons of the Lord. It emerges in our reciprocal relationships, as who we are is disclosed with and for each other. In the family, the final document asserts, "[W]e learn that we are equal in dignity and created for reciprocity" (*For a Synodal Church*, 55).

Chiara Giaccardi: "In Genesis, God creates human beings in His image, male and female. Adam, 'made of dust,' perceives himself as a man only upon seeing Ishà, the woman." And she discovers who she is with him. Giaccardi again: "We are caught between two extremes; on one side, only biology counts, and everything is already written; on the other, biology counts for nothing, and everything can be written at will. Conservatives on one side, progressives on the other. A sterile struggle. . . . The key word is reciprocity, meaning mutual implication and the ability to transform one another, rather than opposing, competing, or claiming. . . . Never without the other, as Michel de Certeau would say."[4]

God gives us the gift of creating each other. All my friends have made me who I am. We are all God's artists! There is a new expression: "You do you." No. We do us.

-highlights/spotlights/2025/the-brutalist-emilia-perez-triumph-at-golden-globes/.

4. Giaccardi, "Reciprocity."

A tiny word of clarification. Reciprocity in this context could be misunderstood as opposed to gratuitous giving: I give you something and in return you give me something back. That is not what I mean. Reciprocity is the free gift of ourselves to each other, through which we both discover who we are.

One of the constant concerns of the synod was the formation of seminarians. How could they discover a wholesome Christian male identity if they are formed in an exclusively male environment without the female other? There is a crisis in the relationship between young men and women in every continent. A study looked at a number of countries on, I think, five continents, and everywhere, regardless of religion or ethnicity, young men and women are finding it harder to relate to each other.[5] Young men are becoming more conservative and young women more liberal. It is becoming ever harder for friendships to form between the sexes and for marriages to endure. It is one factor in the decline of the birth rate in nearly all countries outside of Africa. The future of humanity depends on our finding a liberating vision of what it means to be male and female. Young

5. See, for example, "Why Young Men and Women Are Drifting Apart," *The Economist*, March 13, 2024, https://www.economist.com/international/2024/03/13/why-the-growing-gulf-between-young-men-and-women.

men often see this in terms of complementarity, which traps women in predetermined relationships. They are uncomfortable with women in equal positions in the office. Young women often see this in terms of identity as chosen and constructed. But identity is discovered with and for each other. Toxic masculinity is everywhere on the rise, with resulting violence to women. This is surely the fruit of a crisis of masculinity and of femininity.

Priests can only embody a Christian life if they discover what it is to be male with and from women. And what about women? How in religious communities of women is identity discovered with and for the other, including the male other? The idea of the Dominican family has been present in some form since the beginning of the Order. Dominic clearly loved the company of women. I suspect he preferred living with women to living with his brethren!

He founded a community of women in Prouille before the first community of men was established. Lay Dominicans go back to the very beginning of our tradition. Saint Catherine of Siena's group of friends, the *caterenati*, included men and women. Jordan of Saxony and Diana degli Andalò clearly loved each other, as did Catherine and Blessed Raymond of Capua. The relationship between women and men is part of our Dominican DNA. You cannot be a Dominican and flee the other sex. We are not angels, but bodily men and women.

This can be difficult, especially if one branch of the Order finds another provocative and horribly conservative or alarmingly traditionalist! But the Dominican family is not about belonging to nice, easy, progressive people who think like we do. If Dominic reached out to the Albigensians, we can reach out to our brothers or sisters with whom we disagree and talk to them! And if they do not want to talk, at least let's have a drink! So the Dominican family has something to offer the Church, as we search to understand the reciprocity of the sexes.

What does this say about the question of the ordination of women to the diaconate? Again, being lay or ordained are not fixed, predetermined identities but are discovered reciprocally, with and for each other.

Given the shortage of time, perhaps I could be forgiven for sharing my personal experience. I joined the Order because I wished to be one of the brethren. I was uneasy at the prospect of ordination. When I was ordained, my parents' parish priest, who had condemned those "heretical Dominicans," came and flung himself on the floor before me, wanting to kiss the sacred hands. I fled to my room in horror. I only came down because a German Dominican followed me and wanted to talk about Heidegger, which was even worse.

My embrace of priesthood came through hearing confessions. Here are two sinners sitting beside each other. I shared the mercy of God we both needed. The role of the priest is to be the forgiven sinner who therefore can say to another, "*We* dare to call God 'Our Father.'" The bishop and priest have the ministry of unity, the "we" of the community. They cannot exercise that ministry unless their own identity is stretched open by the people of God, lay men and women. Hence, again, the utter necessity of a formation for seminarians and religious that liberates us from any narrow toxic male or female identity. I give thanks that my first boss as a priest was Sister Gerry, at More House in London, famed for her parties and love of fast motorbikes!

The theme of ministries is utterly pivotal to the synod's final document. The word occurs 108 times. This is not a way of evading the question of the ordination of women. Wow, you can be a lector! How exciting! Who wants to be a deacon when you can be an acolyte? No, the language of ministries opens a space in which it is possible to talk about the reciprocity of roles exercised by the whole people of God, in which everyone has a vocation to pasture the flock. We are all pastors and all sheep.

So the question of the ordination of women involves two sorts of reciprocal roles: of women and men, and of ordained and lay. I suspect that is why Pope Francis thinks the question is open but not yet mature. Because we are still on the way to discovering what these reciprocal relationships mean. Personally, I think that we are ready now. As our brother Cardinal Jean-Paul Vesco said, when asked about this question, "What seems unimaginable today will become natural tomorrow."[6]

This brings me briefly to my final and most important point. For synodality to succeed, we need language that is always being renewed by reciprocity. First of all, fertile thought needs at least two perceptions in fruitful tension with each other! The Church refused to have just one gospel but four which are in tension with each other. When a bishop tried to explain this to a group of prisoners, one said, "Of course they disagree. If they all said the same thing, it would be a put-up job!"

The history of the Church is of the unending dialogue between four gospels. As a character in one of John Berger's novels said, "Never again shall a single story be told as though it were the only one."[7]

The New Testament presents the relationship between men and women in at least two ways. In Galatians, Paul proclaims, "There is no longer Jew or Greek, there is no longer slave or free, there is no longer male and female" (3:28), but also, in Ephesians, as the Body of Christ in

6. "Women Deacons: 'What Seems Unimaginable Today Will Become Natural Tomorrow,' Says Archbishop," *LaCroix International*, May 28, 2024, https://international.la-croix.com/opinions/women-deacons-what-seems-unimaginable-today-will-become-natural-tomorrow-says-archbishop.

7. *G.: A Novel* (Viking Press, 1972), 129.

which there are different vocations, some are called to "be apostles, some prophets, some evangelists, some pastors and teachers" (4:11). These are at least two images that are always in thought-provoking tension.

Most preachers dread the Sunday when the Lectionary gives us Ephesians 5, in which wives are told they must be obedient to their husbands. What can we say? Let's hope the lector speaks very quietly. But right at the beginning, there is that extraordinary statement, "Be subject to one another out of reverence for Christ" (5:21). This tiny seed of reciprocity is sown in this world of Roman patriarchy. This little yeast of reciprocal mutuality is still at work, and we do not know where it will take us.

When two images are in tension with each other, the temptation is to drop one. A delightful Irish journalist whom I met at the synod said that though she loved what *Lumen Gentium* said about the Church as the people of God, she could make nothing of the language of hierarchy. Drop it. That would be like seeking liberation from patriarchy by denying any difference between men and women.

Legend has it that Saint Thomas Aquinas said, "*Hominem unius libri timeo*" ("I fear the person of a single book").[8] It is this singleness of vision that is characteristic of modernity. It tends to literalism and religious fundamentalism. The culture of encounter includes the

8. Jeremy Taylor, *Life of Christ*, pt. II., sect. XII, disc. XII, 16.

encounter of ways of seeing that are not easily compatible, and this tension is only fertile if we are open to poetry and metaphor. Without these there is no culture. Monocultures are ecologically dead.

A reciprocal conversation is one in which words take fire from each other. Key words develop their meaning through the interplay of imaginations. We shall never fully understand words such as *love*, *communion*, *identity*, *mystery*. We go on understanding them as if for the first time. T. S. Eliot wrote:

> We shall not cease from exploration
> And the end of all our exploring
> Will be to arrive where we started
> And know the place for the first time.[9]

Saint Jerome advised us that some Hebrew words, such as *amen* and *alleluia*, should never be translated.[10] The word *mercy* has traveled a long way since Aristotle dismissed it as characteristic of children and old women![11] In the synod, we were not just talking to each other but discovering how to talk, reciprocally rejuvenat-

9. T. S. Eliot, "Little Gidding" (1942), https://www.columbia.edu/itc/history/winter/w3206/edit/tseliotlittlegidding.html.

10. See Saint Jerome, Epistle 26 to Marcella.

11. See Ceslas Spicq, "ἐλεέω, ἔλεοςt," *Theological Lexicon of the New Testament*, trans. James D. Ernest (Tyndale House, 1994).

ing old words and discovering new words that opened our minds and hearts to the Kingdom.

Let me conclude with a simple example. A Japanese lay woman told me that at her table she discovered how different our Western ways of talking are from hers. She said that the Japanese easily say *we*. At the heart of their culture is harmony, *wa*, a key word in the final document. Disagreement is painful and suppressed, buried in silence. But she saw that in the debates of the synod, Westerners often say *I* easily but found it harder to embrace a communal identity and say *we*. In a healthy conversation, I need to say *we*, and we need to let each person say *I*. So around the table, we were teaching each other how to speak. All this was difficult to communicate in the final document, which is not intercultural but written in Italian and largely by Italians, excellent though it is.

So the task of the synod does not conclude with this "final" document or even with the reports of the study groups. It is an imaginative task in which we can all be engaged, as we refresh our mutuality in words open to the infinite mystery of God's love. Every renewal of the Church is surely also an aesthetic renaissance. Gregorian chant, baroque art, Wesleyan hymnody—all were midwives to renewed imaginations, new ways of being together in the Lord. This is what it means to be disciples of the one whose name revealed to Moses can be translated as "I will be who I will be."

Between a Rock and a Hard Place[1]

A week ago, there was a knock on the door of my study. A young university student wanted to talk to me about a concern. He loves and admires Pope Francis, but he said that many young Catholics of his generation longed for a clear teaching of the doctrines of the Catholic faith. He was missing Pope Benedict. In this uncertain world, some people want clarity. He admired the beautiful openness of the Holy Father and the welcome that he gives to everyone, but thought that we need clear teaching and a strong moral vision. I hear similar demands from lots of people everywhere.

Jesus is a teacher. He said to the disciples just before his death, "You call me Teacher and Lord—and you are

1. This is a talk given to pastoral workers in the diocese of Liege, Belgium, March 2025.

right, for that is what I am" (John 13:13). With the last words of Matthew's gospel, the disciples are sent to teach all the nations of the earth (Matt 28). A disciple is someone who is taught and who teaches.

How, then, are we to teach our faith today? Our society is deeply suspicious of all doctrine and dogma. Accepting dogma looks like a renunciation of freedom of thought. As Steve Jobs said in his commencement speech at Stanford: "Your time is limited, so don't waste it living someone else's life. Don't be trapped by dogma—which is living with the results of other people's thinking."[2]

Many people are happy with Christianity as a spirituality, even as an ethical vision. Many people claim to be "cultural Christians" but Christian doctrine is considered either with suspicion or as irrelevant. But there are many young people who are hungry for clear teaching, like this student who knocked on my door. How, then, are we to teach?

Cardinal Suhard, who was archbishop of Paris, said that "one of the priest's first services to the world is to tell the truth."[3] We must proclaim the truth of the gospel and the teachings of the Church. But we must also be true

2. " 'You've Got to Find What You Love,' Jobs Says," *Stanford Report*, June 12, 2005, https://news.stanford.edu/stories/2005/06/youve-got-find-love-jobs-says.

3. Quoted in Michael Heher, *The Lost Art of Walking on Water: Reimagining the Priesthood* (Paulist, 2004), 114.

to the complexity of people's lives. When people have a family member who is gay, or transgender, or divorced, what sense does the Church's teaching then make? So we live often in the space between the truths of our faith and the truths of people's brave but difficult lives.

When I began my Dominican studies, my first teacher was a Sri Lankan called Cornelius Ernst. He was a poet, a former Communist, and a disciple of Ludwig Wittgenstein. He fell in love with Catholicism while sitting on a bench in Cambridge. He even showed me the bench. Above all he was captivated by the beautiful coherence of Aquinas's theology. But when he was in his late forties he had a crisis. He fell in love and struggled to make a new sense of his life. Shortly before he died, he wrote in his diary that he was faithful to the Church's teaching but, he added, "I have another tradition to which I am almost equally respectful—in some ways more so—the tradition of the human heart: novels, art, music, tragedy. I cannot allow that God can only be adored in spirit and in truth by the individual introverted upon himself and detached from all that might disturb and solicit his heart. It must be possible to find and adore God in the complexity of human experience."[4] He must be true to both the Church and experience.

4. *Multiple Echo: Explorations in Theology*, ed. Fergus Kerr OP and Timothy Radcliffe OP (Darton, Longman and Todd, 1979), 1.

Father Tony Philpot was one of the most respected diocesan priests in Britain and spiritual director at the English College in Rome. He went to a lecture in Cambridge given by the then Cardinal Ratzinger. It was a wonderful, intelligent lecture. But it seemed remote from what his parishioners were living. He felt torn apart. He wrote, "It is uncomfortable, occupying the space between the rock and the hard place. It is uncomfortable to belong to the world of orthodoxy, and yet spend so much of my time and energy with the unorthodox, and indeed to belong to their world too. I would want to say to men preparing for diocesan priesthood that this divided heart is the characteristic pain of their vocation, and if they experience the pain, it is a sign that they will be good priests."[5]

Good teaching is the fruit of this divided heart. This was the space in which the synod took place, planted in the middle of this tension between the truths of our faith and the truths of people's complex lives. Pope Francis declared that the final document of the synod is "part of the ordinary Magisterium of the Successor of Peter (cf. EC 18 § 1; CCC 892), and as such, I ask that it be welcomed and received. It represents a form of exercise of the authentic teaching of the Bishop of Rome."[6] Its

5. *Priesthood in Reality: Living the Vocation of a Diocesan Priest in a Changing World* (Bury St Edmunds, 1998), 88.

6. "Accompanying Note by the Holy Father Francis," in *For a Synodal Church*, 3.

authority derives from its double fidelity, to the gospel and to the hopes and sufferings of the people of God.

It is in this space that God is encountered, as God dwells in the space between the wings of the cherubim over the ark—or the empty space of a tomb on Easter morning. The center of our teaching is a man suspended between heaven and earth on a cross, whose last words were a question, according to Saints Mark and Matthew.

This is the space that we priests occupy as teachers. It is a tough place to be because some people insist on a clarity which can blind us to God's presence in our daily struggles, and others dismiss the Church's teaching as irrelevant or outdated. Some people claim to know everything with alarming certainty, and others are torn apart by doubt. I am reminded of the words of the Irish poet W. B. Yeats, written after the First World War devastated Belgium:

> The best lack all conviction, while the worst
> Are full of passionate intensity.[7]

How, then, are we to live this tension and teach the faith? First of all, with compassion. In the gospels, Jesus' teaching was an act of compassion. Mark tells us that before the feeding of the five thousand, when Jesus saw the great

7. "The Second Coming," https://www.poetryfoundation.org/poems/43290/the-second-coming.

throng of people, "he had compassion for them, because they were like sheep without a shepherd; and he began to *teach* them many things" (6:34). Compassionate teaching feeds them. According to the Catholic tradition, teaching is an act of spiritual mercy. All teaching and preaching springs from compassion for people's lives and struggles.

A Dominican novice master of my Province said a hundred years ago, "Love those to whom you preach. If you do not, don't preach to them. Preach to yourself." So we shall only be good teachers if we open our hearts to all that they live. We, in a sense, have to become one of them, and know their puzzlement and failures from within—as God became one of us "in all things except sin."

Inhabiting that space between a rock and a hard place, between the Church's teaching and the lives of our people, means making their questions our own. We must not think that teaching is just giving people the answers to their questions. An archbishop told a meeting of Dominican novices that they should study Aquinas's *Summa* because it gave fifty-six thousand answers to all the questions they would ever encounter. Saint Thomas would have been scandalized!

Teaching begins when we dare to embrace the questions that burn in people's hearts and make them somehow our own in prayer and thought. Tomaš Halik says that Saint Thérèse of Lisieux's difficult vocation was to be united with atheists. Nineteenth-century France was rabid with anticlericalism, and indeed atheism, but this was her home. He says, "Thérèse declares that she *perceives unbelievers as her brothers*, with whom she *sits at the same table and eats the same bread*—and she begs Jesus not to banish her therefrom."[8] She wanted to be in solidarity with these disbelievers, and drink their cup of pain, share their questions as she prayed to God. Then real compassionate teaching can begin.

Teaching is inseparable from embracing the questions to which one has no immediate answer. I wrote a book, *Interroger Dieu*, with a young Polish Dominican called Łukasz Popko, who teaches at the École Biblique in Jerusalem.[9] It contains eighteen conversations between us about God and humanity in the Bible. What we had not realized at the beginning was that almost all of the conversations revolve around questions, either God's questions to humanity or human questions to God. The first conversation in the Bible begins with God's question to Adam: "Where are you?" One of the last we consider is Jesus' question to Simon Peter: "Do you love me more than these others?" Jacob asks another stranger: "What is your name?" God asks Elijah on Mount Horeb, "What are you doing here?"

8. *Patience with God: The Story of Zacchaeus Continuing in Us*, trans. Gerard Turner (Doubleday, 2009), 29.

9. Les Éditions du Cerf, 2024.

Why is the Bible filled with so many questions? Certainly, when God asks questions—"Where are you, Adam?"—it is not because God needs information. Profound questions invite us to enter a new way of being. The best questions invite us to live more profoundly! Rainer Maria Rilke wrote, "Do not now seek the answers, which cannot be given you, because you would not be able to live them. And the point is, to live everything. *Live* the questions now. Perhaps you will then gradually, without noticing it, live along some distant day into the answer."[10]

Profound questions beckon us to become alive in a new way. The synod's main purpose was not to find answers but to invite the Church to choose life again and again. Legend tells us that as a child Saint Thomas Aquinas asked the question, "What is God?" He went on asking that question all of his life and could never answer it. Thomas's holiness was to live with the question and refuse all of the wrong answers. Thomas could only have a tiny taste of who God is by sharing God's life in grace. Yes, we can make true statements about God, such as that God is one, true, and beautiful. But, he said, we cannot fully understand what they mean since we do not grasp what it means for God to be God.

10. *Letters to a Young Poet*, rev. ed., trans. N. D. Herter Norton (Norton, 1954), Letter 4, July 16, 1903.

So the truths of our faith are not cold facts but expressions of lived grace. Saint John writes in his first letter, "God abides in those who confess that Jesus is the Son of God, and they abide in God. So we have known and believe the love that God has for us. God is love, and those who abide in love abide in God, and God abides in them" (4:15-16). If we abide in the questions and let them probe our hearts and minds, we shall abide in the Lord.

I was rather a bad boy at my Benedictine school. I was always escaping to go to the pub or buy cigarettes. I was almost expelled from school. I considered myself a Catholic, like all of my family. But I had not deeply grasped my faith. The turning point was when I left school and began to make friends with non-Catholics. One of them said to me: "Timothy, the Catholic Church teaches things which are not true." This became for me the great question. Are these teachings true or not?

But the answer is not just yes or no. It is becoming alive in a new way, for me a Dominican way. The motto of our Order is *Veritas*, Truth. Believing in the Trinity, for example, is not just celestial mathematics. It is entering into the mystery of a love which is utterly relational, equal, and eternal. That is a love which challenges us every day to share the life of the Triune God. The doctrine of the Trinity is the most down-to-earth, practical doctrine imaginable. Belief in the resurrection is not just a claim about something that happened to a dead body two thousand years ago, though it *is* that. It opens a new way to be alive now in the face of death.

So, all teaching is the invitation to live. In Deuteronomy, God says to Israel, "I have set before you life and death. . . . Choose life" (30:19). An Anglican priest, Mark Oakley, wrote, "For the Christian, death is not the worst thing. Not living your life is the worst thing. We always need others to help us achieve that."[11] For me, the deep pleasure of our little book *Interroger Dieu* was that we lived these questions together. It was a delight that we are so different. Łukasz is half my age and twice as intelligent. He is one of the best experts on Hebrew in the world. I am a preacher who has wandered around the world for a long time.

During the synod it was noted that priests and bishops often complain of loneliness and isolation. One of the ways that we overcome loneliness is by sharing the deepest questions in our hearts. Not just so as to find answers but because this *is* the heart of friendship. C. S. Lewis said that lovers look at each other, but friends look in the same direction. They may disagree with each other, but at least they share some of the same questions. I quote: "'Do you *care about* the same truth?' The [one] who agrees with us that some question, little regarded

11. *The Splash of Words: Believing in Poetry* (Canterbury Press, 2016), 49.

by others, is of great importance can be our Friend. He need not agree with us about the answer."[12]

So we should dare to share with our fellow priests our deepest questions, even our doubts and failures. Then we shall help each other to become teachers. I had a good friend, Gareth, with whom I loved to argue. For Gareth the point of arguing was not for him to win but for the truth to win. He gave a lecture on Saint Paul's sexual ethics in which he criticized an article that I had written. Some people said, "Be careful. Timothy might be the next Provincial." I felt honored that he thought it worth disagreeing with me. Afterward we went to the pub together, a good Dominican tradition since the Order was founded in a pub!

Life-giving questions take us out of our depth. As Saint John Paul II wrote at the beginning of the millennium, *Duc in altum*: "Go out into the deep." Then we shall have to beg for help so that we do not drown. We shall pray to the Lord for illumination. We shall ask for the help of any wise person, whether they share our faith or not. Saint Dominic wanted his brethren to be beggars. Not just for food but for the bread of truth. Like Philip at the feeding of the five thousand, we shall ask, "How shall we feed the people?" (see John 6:5). The disciples had so little, just five loaves and a couple of fish. We may find that as teachers

12. *The Four Loves* (Harcourt Brace, 1991), 66.

we have few words and lots of questions, like the disciples. But if our words are true—true to the gospel and true to what people live—and compassionate, they will be enough for the moment. An American Dominican, William Hill, said, "God cannot do without the stammering ways in which we strive to give utterance to that Word."[13] It is better to give a badly expressed half answer that is true than an eloquent, brilliant answer that is not lived.

God often chooses as his prophets people who struggle to find words. Think of Moses! Moses said to the Lord, "O my Lord, I have never been eloquent, neither in the past nor even now that you have spoken to your servant; but I am slow of speech and slow of tongue" (Exod 4:10). Or Jeremiah, who stammers: " 'Ah, Lord God! Truly I do not know how to speak, for I am only a boy.' But the Lord said to me, 'Do not say, "I am only a boy"; for you shall go to all to whom I send you, and you shall speak whatever I command you' " (1:6-7).

So, a good teacher should sometimes be lost for words, and overcome by a sense that we do not know what to say. That is how God likes it, as long as our few words are true and compassionate. When it was necessary, the Lord sent Aaron to stammering Moses to help him speak.

13. "Preaching as a 'Moment' in Theology," in *Search for the Absent God: Tradition and Modernity in Religious Understanding*, ed. Mary Catherine Hilkert (Crossroad, 1992), 186.

Jesus says to the disciples: "When they bring you to trial and hand you over, do not worry beforehand about what you are to say; but say whatever is given you at that time, for it is not you who speak, but the Holy Spirit" (Mark 13:11). This does not mean that we do not prepare. We pray, we study, we read, we ask. But what we are to say will be given in that hour when we see people's faces and look them in the eyes. If it is of the Holy Spirit it will be true and compassionate, even if we have not much to say and are unable to say it well.

We truly become alive when we abide patiently with profound questions that haunt the human heart. We simultaneously hold onto truths which seem to be incompatible, hoping to discover some reconciliation. When we want to say contradictory things, then our teaching becomes interesting. In the sequel to *Alice's Adventures in Wonderland*, the White Queen boasts that she says at least six impossible things before breakfast every day! If we abide in the truth with compassion, then we shall meet God, even if only, as Meister Eckhart said, like hearing a cough in the dark.[14]

14. "It is just as if a man were to hide himself and then to give himself away by clearing his throat: God has done the same." "Sermon Ninety-One," in *The Complete Mystical Works of Meister Eckhart*, trans. Maurice O'C. Walshe (Crossroad, 2009), 447.

A Jewish student went to see a rabbi to ask him a question. The rabbi asked him, "What is your question?" The student replied, "What is the essence of truth?" The rabbi looked at him and slapped him hard. The student retreated, upset. Then one of the rabbi's students came and said to him that this was a kindness of the rabbi. He was teaching you this: "never surrender a good question for a mere answer."[15]

We may have to wait a long time for that word to be given to us. As the poet T. S. Eliot wrote, "the faith and the love and the hope are all in the waiting."[16] We wait like Elijah on the mountain, and God is not in the wind of the teachers who have lots of windy words. God is not in the earthquake of people who want to shake up everything, nor in the hellfire sermons of those who condemn everyone, but in "a thin whisper, silence," as Łukasz Popko translates it. So often the Church has lost authority because we have not waited until the Lord has spoken quietly, but have rushed in with premature answers. Sound teaching matures slowly like old wine.

Two things follow from this. First, we should look to all people who struggle to understand the great questions of human existence as possible allies. The painter Paul

15. Oakley, *Splash of Words*, 87.

16. "Wait Without Hope," https://allpoetry.com/poem/17577554-Wait-Without-Hope-by-T-S-Eliot.

Gauguin left the Church and the Church denounced him. But his most famous painting was called *D'où venons-nous ? Que sommes-nous ? Où allons-nous ?* "Where Do We Come From? What Are We? Where Are We Going?" These were the first three questions of his catechism when he was a teenager. The questions remained even when he left the Church. What might have happened if the Church had tried to accompany him in his searching instead of rejecting him? The Church and Gauguin both might have been the richer.

Secondly, the great challenge to our preaching is not atheism but superficiality, boredom. Jason Blakely wrote, "The deadliest poison in human life is not anger but boredom. A boredom that contains the most thorough rejection of existence. A mocking, lazy, listless, proud, ugly and spiteful boredom that looks at the whole of being, its shimmering grandeur, its never-spent newness, and says a single word: *no.*"[17] Superficiality and reductionism are the temptations of our age, the flood of so many vacuous words on social media.

How are we to touch people bogged down in superficiality, forever tapping their iPhones? One way is to be alive in ways that are puzzling. I hope people will ask why we are so joyful, even playful.

17. "An Atheist's Return to the Catholic Church: A Story of Death, Love and Meaning," *America*, December 9, 2024.

The Cistercian monk Thomas Merton gave his last lecture in Bangkok just before he died, electrocuted in the shower. After the lecture he spoke with a religious sister who asked why he had not tried to convert his hearers to Christianity. His last-known words were: "I think today it's more important for us to so let God live in us that others may feel God and come to believe in God because they feel how God lives in us."[18] We should be alive with a joy that intrigues people. Then they will want to know what our secret is. On the morning of Pentecost, people thought that the disciples who had received the Spirit were drunk. How odd! Then the teaching began.

18. From a lecture by Sister Mary Luke Tobin, quoted in Beth Cioffoletti, "Merton's Last Words," *louie, louie* (blog), December 10, 2012, https://fatherlouie.blogspot.com/2012/12/mertons-last-words.html.

SURPRISED BY HOPE